HEALING OF REJECTION
WITH THE HELP OF THE LORD

HEALING OF REJECTION WITH THE HELP OF THE LORD

—*A Survivor's Guide*—

Ronda Chervin

⊕ ENROUTE

En Route Books & Media
5705 Rhodes Avenue, St. Louis, MO 63109
Contact us at contactus@enroutebooksandmedia.com
Find En Route online at www.enroutebooksandmedia.com

LCCN: 2016960340

Cover design by TJ Burdick
Cover image credits:

lauragrafie, Remember December, via flikr CC:
https://flic.kr/p/kEXTJL

McGrath, Sean, A Portrait in Darkness, via flikr CC:
https://flic.kr/p/61FhnR

Paperback ISBN: 978-1-950108-48-0
E-book ISBN: 978-1-63337-143-9

Printed in the United States of America

—CONTENTS—

FOREWORD

Standing on a street corner in East Texas with some friends back in my teenage years, I was introduced to a new game called "Denied!" One reached over to me for a high-five, and I responded in kind only to see his hand fly up to groom his hair and hear the exclamation, "Denied!" We all laughed, and the game made its course through various other groups of my friends—sometimes instigated by me—for the next several months. The joke was in finding someone who hadn't yet been introduced to it so that person could be shocked when "Denied!"

What does it do to us to think we are a part of something only to have the proverbial rug pulled out from under us, even teasingly, and told, especially within the context of a group setting, that we've been denied the pleasure, indeed the expectation, of an interpersonal bond? Most of us can think of real instances where we've been "Denied!" from one thing or another through the actions or inactions of another person. And the more we fixate on it, the more it can affect our self-image, whether we envision ourselves in private or in various group contexts. We start to apply meanings to these little rejections that were perhaps never intended by those who rejected us.

"She doesn't want me near her because I'm too fat!"— well, maybe she just feels fat herself.

"He doesn't want me to bring my son over for the holidays because he's disappointed in the choices I made in life!" —well, maybe he feels guilty that there's something he might have done at one point in his life that would have changed the options, and he didn't do it.

"He still affirms me professionally but no longer comments on my looks, so I must have become ugly or plain to him!"—well, maybe he realizes he's become too attracted to those looks and has to pull back for fear of falling into an affair.

"Daddy won't play with me because he would rather work!"—well, maybe daddy just has work and can't organize his schedule very well.

The fact is that there are all kinds of reasons we have for denying others, but when we're on the receiving end of a denial—when we're on the receiving end of rejection—we fixate on some deficit, some lack of something, within us. And it can profoundly affect our sense of self and our relationships with others—including our relationship with God.

So, how do we heal? There are as many ways for healing as there are ways to feel rejected because our expectations are higher than reality. Dr. Ronda in the pages of this book provides a good framework for us to understand this healing process through the art of story-telling and testimonials. When she first asked me to review her book, I said, "Sure!" and resisted the temptation to follow-up with a "Denied!" I'm glad I did!

—Dr. Sebastian Mahfood, OP,
Professor of Interdisciplinary Studies,
Holy Apostles College & Seminary

INTRODUCTION

Feeling rejected is one of the most painful of experiences. In the case of childhood rejection by parents, often the emotions of that time are not consciously remembered until later. In the case of rejection by a lover, for instance, the pain is most poignantly related to its cause. Why else would songs, whether country-western or operatic, about rejection by a boyfriend, girlfriend, or spouse, be so universally identified with?

In the past, feeling rejected led me to the brink of suicide. Psychotherapists have helped me survive such agonizing times. Ultimately it is the experience of God's perfect love that has brought me through crisis after crisis to the point where I am now able to cope with the miseries of human rejection to emerge with hope and, even, joy. More than ever, now, I can trace the patterns of fantasy, anxiety, and despair that have brought so much unhappiness in my life.

I wrote this small book, *Healing of Rejection with the Help of the Lord: A Survivor's Guide*, to help you to move out of the disordered bondings that so often accompany rejection. I am praying that your reading will lead you into a surrender to the God of love with rebirth and healing.

If God graces this effort, the result should be that we will all resonate with St. Paul's description of love: "Love is patient, kind, not jealous or boastful…does not insist on its own way; it is not irritable or resentful…bears all things, believes all things, endures all things…never ends." (1 Corinthians 13:4-8)

At first, you may find my format disconcerting. I will be using three fictional stories to lead you into consideration of the pathos of rejection. You will come to know six people indulging in seemingly harmless fantasies; suffering the anxieties that come when they want more from others than anyone can deliver; and then experiencing despair when relationships capsize. Finally my heroes and heroines will surrender to God. Temptations to disordered cycles will be overcome after much struggle. Real tender love, sustained by ongoing forgiveness, will be the victor.

After the narratives, I will move on to analysis of the main theme of each chapter. For ease in writing and your reading I am putting only the title of cited books in the body of the text with the page number. Bibliographical information will be at the end of this book.

Will you join in this opening prayer?

Dear Jesus, prince of peace, you long to liberate us from the pain of rejection. Heal us from wounds that trap us in self-defeating patterns. Pour your love into our hearts so that our bondings may become more life-giving.

Fantasy

"The heart is a most wild beast
and makes many a light leap."
Anonymous Medieval Dominican priest

Lynn and Pete

My first story is about Lynn and Pete. Lynn is a forty-two-year-old, good-looking blonde woman separated from her husband, Bill. They have two teenage children. Pete is the manager of a furniture store in Phoenix. Lynn works at the store in the accounting department. Pete is married to Joy. They have four young children.

The face in the glass—not young, but, what? Piquant? Sweet?... Even a little attractive? Sure better today than any other day since I turned that dread age of forty!

Lynn winked at herself in the mirror. *Because of Pete*, she mused. Lynn shrugged off a slightly anxious feeling and asked herself defensively, *Why shouldn't it be nice to have a boss who smiles at me for a change?*

When big Pete, with the sparkling eyes, dark curly hair, and a big smile, arrived last month to take over as manager, Lynn warmed up to him right away. She liked the fact that instead of waiting for a formal introduction, he sat down on her desk and looked at the photo of her kids. Her previous grouchy boss called her Lynn but insisted on her calling him Mr. Block. This new one told her from the get-go to call him Pete.

Today, on her drive home from work, Lynn wondered if Pete had noticed that she wasn't wearing a wedding ring. She remembered the lunch they had enjoyed together at the Mario's restaurant. They were celebrating the increased sales figures for Pete's first month managing the store. It felt so good to be out with a man who could have a good time without getting drunk the way her ex, Bill, always did at restaurants.

Two years separated. I'm not sorry, but I guess I do feel lonely.

Just before falling asleep that night Lynn pictured big handsome Pete approaching her as she was trying out a new sofa in the show room. She imagined him sitting down and putting an arm around her shoulder.

Meanwhile, late afternoon, driving home to his wife, Joy, and the kids, Pete thought, *Funny how the image of that blonde, nicely-shaped assistant of mine, Lynn, keeps haunting me. She doesn't dress sexy like some of the other gals at work. Keeps to herself mostly. Tony Korzi, the regional president, mentioned that she was separated from her husband—some kind of abusive alcoholic. How sad!*

I like the way she smiles whenever I come to her office with the papers from a new sale, or how she caught on so soon to what kind of donut I like for my coffee break.

I'm a happily married family man, for sure, but it can't hurt to show Lynn I appreciate how she brightens my day. That dream last night of me kissing Lynn on the lips; better pray not to have too many of those.

Matt and Joey

Matt, 6'4", thin, of Italian ancestry, is a thirty-five-year-old telephone repairman. He is the dad of Joey, age nine as our story opens. The family lives in Revere, Massachusetts. Matt is the coach of Joey's Little League team. Carol is Joey's mother, and Dee is Joey's older sister.

"Go, Joey, go!"

What a kid! He's circling the bases like a pro, Matt thinks to himself proudly. *I can picture him now...pony league, minor league, farm team, semi-pro...one day, another Babe Ruth, Lou Gehrig, Mark McGwire.*

How I love this game. I thought I'd make it big myself. I wonder if I'll ever forgive that jerk who spiked me coming around second base like it was football. Broke my kneecap. Never got healed up enough to even make the minors.

"Run, Joey, run... That's a boy, grab it, throw it to third! What an arm! That's my boy Joey."

Four years later, Joey was a freshman at high school.

"Sorry, Mrs. Dean, what was the question?" When she asked again about the dates of World War I and he didn't know the answer, Joe thought, *I better pay attention. That "D" on the last math test will be the last straw. Report cards are just a few weeks off. Not that Dad cares if I don't do great as long as I pass.*

Three weeks later, coming home for a snack before baseball practice, Joe's mom confronted him with his C+ report card. She looked sad. "Joe dear, I don't care if you don't get A's like Dee does, but how are you going to get into college with mostly C's?"

Later that night Joe overheard his parents talking during the commercials on their favorite sitcom: *Everybody Loves Raymond.* "Matt, I just can't stand the idea of Joey winding up taking tech courses at the community college because of his high school average. On your salary you know we can't save up for those huge college fees. He'll have to do much better to get a scholarship. I'd be happy to get a job to help. It's you who insists women should stay at home."

"Heck, Carol, how many times have I told you, this boy's gonna have twenty colleges begging him to come and play baseball for them. Stop nagging him."

Joe stopped listening and went upstairs to watch baseball reruns while finishing his homework. As he was falling asleep he told himself, *Mom just doesn't understand. During those boring classes at school, all I can think of is last week's game, the flubs, the hits, the runs, trying to beat out the tricks of the pitchers of the other teams. Well, when I make it big no one will ask how I did at this cruddy high school, that's for sure. I can just picture Dad's face beaming at me when I'm in the big leagues.*

Tom and Cathy

Tom is a stocky Franciscan seminarian of average height with a crew cut. He is doing his intern year in hospital ministry. He wears a long, brown Franciscan habit with a white knotted cord for a belt. Cathy is a short, young woman of twenty-six, with long, red curly hair. She is assistant chaplain at St. Luke's, a Catholic hospital in Corpus Christi, Texas.

Cathy was sitting in the chapel of the hospital taking a prayer break from her rounds. She was half musing and half praying.

Ever since Brother Tom confided in me that he's unsure about going on for the priesthood, I feel so uncomfortable around him. Are you mad at me, Jesus? On my way to bring him to minister to the new patients, instead of praying for him to reach the people in the ward, I picture those large brown eyes of his as they might be looking right into mine, or those gentle hands around my face.

What a great father he would make! I know it's silly, but I've started thinking of names we could give our children if...

This is wrong. Jesus, you want me to hope he'll make it to the priesthood where all the love in his heart can be spread around to everyone, not just me, right?...

Cathy extended her arms toward the crucifix in a gesture of abandonment. Then she remembered the intensely interested look on Brother Tom's face once when she confessed how lonely it was being single.

Now Cathy asked herself, *Was I being flirtatious? Was it my imagination that the loving look in Tom's eyes meant he might want to help me become less lonely someday?*

Tom was praying in the Franciscan Seminary Church near the hospital. *Thank you, God, for my charming friend Cathy. If, after all, I decide you're not calling me to the priesthood, would she be the one you wanted for me?*

Tom could almost feel what it would be like to run his fingers through Cathy's long, curly red hair. He wondered how many boyfriends she'd had. *She's so attractive she must have had many.* He wondered how intimate she had been with them.

Realizing that instead of praying on his knees in an upright position, he was sprawled out on the pew daydreaming, Tom jerked himself into a kneeling position. He remembered what Father John, his spiritual director, had advised him during their last monthly session, "If you're not sure about priesthood, Tom, be very careful to avoid getting close to single women. And never take off the habit no matter where you're invited."

"But Cathy's so holy, Father. It's so inspiring to talk to her. If you met her you'd love her. She's always talking about how the patients hunger for a real live relationship to Jesus."

On his way back to the rectory after his distracted prayer time Tom thought, *I guess it's only human to imagine what it would be like if Cathy were my wife someday.*

—Analysis of Fantasy—

The narratives about our six characters will eventually become stories about rejection. Yet, these tales all begin with fantasies about perfect relationships! Does this mean that our imaginations are our enemies?

Not necessarily. The imagination is one of the basic faculties of the human mind. A day without images coming up on the screen of our minds, flitting about, racing and departing, would be mighty dull as well as abnormal.

We have to be able to picture the future in order to plan for it. The image of the completed work of art guides the artist's hand. A pregnant mother often dreams of the baby she will one day see, usually prompting her to choose a name, and to buy needed furnishings and baby clothing. Fantasies of what heaven will be like, including our eternal encounter with Jesus, Mary, Joseph, the angels and the saints, and our beloved dead, give wings to the soul of an aging Christian confined to a bed.

It is natural to have fantasies about what could happen in relationships. Matt dreams of his son's successful future in baseball and the joys they will experience together over those victories. Lynn and Pete or Tom and Cathy picture what could happen as they bond with each other. Flashing images, even of actions that are not moral in present circumstances, cannot be totally repressed even if they should be controlled.

I have written the opening narratives about our six characters in such a way that their fantasies can be seen as natural rather than portends of tragedy or sin. At the same time, the reader will guess that these seemingly harmless images can become dangerous or unhealthy. Rejection lurks.

How so? Clearly there is nothing wrong about seeing the

intrinsic worth of another person and appreciating their virtues and talents. We are all created in the image of God. At their best, all people are wonderful. But are we always at our best? Disappointed spouses often tell me that they must have been blind to marry such flawed individuals. I reply that what they saw when they were in love was really there. It's just that most people don't live most of the time at their best. A marital choice should be based on the other person's average, not on his or her highest moments of beauty or virtue.

Here is a telling passage from the old classic Lorna Doone:

> "For nine women out of ten must have some kind of romance or other, to make their lives endurable; and when their love has lost this attractive element, this soft dew-fog, the love itself is apt to languish; unless its bloom be well replaced by the budding hopes of children." (p. 402)

Consider another aspect of fantasy. How close might our fictional characters be to thinking the loved one is the most perfect person in the world? Without faults? Or, only the most minor shortcomings? How soon might these loved ones become idols in the sense of seeming more important even than God? The more perfect the fantasy, the more painful the rejection! We don't mind so much if a stranger who pumps our gas stops smiling at us one day. But, if the other has become god-like, then rejection can seem unbearable!

You might ask yourself at this point whether in your own life innocent relationships that seemed on their way to total happiness, instead turned out to be among the most painful.

This passage from the writings of John Paul the Great explains more about deeper theological implications of having too active a fantasy life:

> "As a result of denying original sin, many contemporary people, after having rejected the faith on this matter, are unable to find reasons for the mysterious and anguishing implications of the evil experienced daily and 'end by oscillating between hasty and irresponsible optimism and a radical and desperate pessimism.'"
>
> John Paul II

ANXIETY

We will return now to our characters, taking into account a passage of time since the last narratives.

Lynn and Pete

On the way home from work, Lynn was thinking about Pete.

This is the second week Pete cancelled our usual Friday lunch date. His reasons made sense—taking the older kids to the dentist so his wife, Joy, could stay home with a sick little one; needing to use lunch hour to fill out a passport application.

Still, it could be something else. Maybe he's feeling guilty about our friendship. We've never done anything wrong in the year since he started working here… Lori, the assistant manag-

er, looked at us kind of funny when she saw us together at Mario's a few weeks ago. I hope she didn't notice that I blushed.

I felt a little uncertain about buying him a birthday present. It took a little doing—searching through the personal data forms on the personnel manager's computer to find out when Pete's birthday was. I did it after closing time. His birthday turned out to be just a few weeks off. I found a cheap CD of Chopin études because I remembered he once said the Polish composer was his favorite. I left the gift on his desk the night before his birthday. When I passed by the next morning it was not there, but he never said thank you. He's usually so polite. On my way to the restroom later on, I checked his desk to see if he had opened my present. It wasn't there In the mirror in the bathroom I could see my face had reddened.

Should I remind him about our Friday lunch next Thursday? Maybe I shouldn't. Just leave it to him? The idea that he might just drop our relationship makes me feel nervous in the stomach, all jittery. It would be so awkward to have to see him every day if he decides to reject me.

Lynn felt a guilty shame when she recalled how often she would give into the fantasy that Pete's wife might die suddenly in an accident, and how happy she might be as Pete's second wife!

On Saturday, Pete was home working on the rock garden and watching out for the little kids. Joy was out doing the weekly grocery shopping. Pete found his mind wandering to thoughts of Lynn.

She looked sort of hurt when I wished her a good week-end. I guess she expected a response to her sweet birthday gift last Monday. I was about to walk into her office and give her a thank you hug, but then something stopped me. My guardian angel? Ha! Haven't thought of him since we were kids saying that prayer every morning on the way out the door for school. How did it go? Angel dear, my guardian...

Well, I have started getting a little more cautious. After all, she's separated from her husband. Never talks about dating other guys. Her teen sons are probably not home most of the time. She must be lonely. It wouldn't be good if having lunch with the boss became the highlight of her week.

Yeah. I guess I better cool it. Maybe take her out to a thank you lunch for all her help from time to time, but not regularly. People at work could talk.

Matt and Joey

It was Joey's junior year at high school. He had just turned seventeen, and was dating a cute cheerleader, Marcy. Joe was the star of the baseball team, as usual.

To everyone's surprise, that March Joey began to skip lunch hour in the cafeteria to work with the art teacher on extracurricular projects. First it was a mural for the school auditorium depicting the landing of the pilgrims. Next it was an entry for a competition with drawings of how Boston might look fifty years in the future.

During the TV commercials one evening, Joe's mom, Carol, was talking to his father, Matt: "I think it's great the way Joe is taking an interest in something besides baseball for a change."

"Sure, another Michelangelo in the making," Matt sneered.

"Come on, Matt. You were there when Ms. Rodney showed us his drawings. She thinks Joe's gonna win a prize at the art show. She thought he might even want to major in art in college."

"Look, Carol, we've been through this before. Joey's a natural pitcher. By the way, I want you to tell him that once a week is plenty to date that chick. Don't want him all tired out at practice from checking her out."

After the next sequence in their favorite sitcom, Carol insisted that Matt turn around and pay attention. "Listen up, Matt, just because you wanted to be a baseball star doesn't mean that Joe has to be!"

Matt grunted but didn't reply.

At one of the play-off games that spring, Matt found himself sitting in the bleachers cracking his knuckles, a habit he had dropped in his twenties when Carol objected to it.

What's the matter with the kid? Still hitting okay but his pitching is off. They're going to lose this game if he doesn't start putting more English on the ball.

That afternoon Joe's team lost by two points because of a home run by the opposing team in the last inning. On the way to the parking lot Matt didn't say anything. Neither did Joe. The father drove right past the Sizzler where they usually celebrated—if not a win, at least Joe's great pitching.

Back home, while Joe was heating up a frozen burger in the microwave, his sister, Dee, noticed his glum face.

"Ran into Marcy at the mall, Joey," Dee grinned. "She forced me to have a smoothie with her so she could quiz me about you."

"Yeah, like what did she wanna know?" Joe brightened.

"You know—how many girlfriends you had before her… whether you were dreaming of going out of town to college."

Joe sat down across from Dee to eat his late dinner. Joe asked his sister, "Tell me more about Boston College. What do you know about the art department?"

Hearing the heavy tread of his dad coming down the stairs toward the kitchen, Joe put his forefinger over his lip to signal his sister that his interest in art was a taboo subject with their father.

Tom and Cathy

Brother Tom stood in front of his three-foot-high clothing closet at the seminary, looking at his Franciscan robe, and then at two shirts, a pair of jeans, and his overalls. I'm not doing ministry, it's just a social occasion, he reasoned as he donned the white shirt and the jeans. Cathy had invited him to a party at her house.

After asking a few questions about his relationship to Cathy, Father Sebastian, the Franciscan in charge of permissions said, "Okay, but only stay a short while; maybe Jesus wants you to reach out to someone there." Then he added, "If there's drinking don't take more than one."

When Tom arrived at the party, the room was filled with young people, most with beer cans in their hands. As soon as Cathy noticed Tom, she pushed through the crowd to greet him. Next to her was a tall, handsome young man. "Brother Tom, heh! Thanks for coming. I want you to meet my boyfriend, Alex."

After Cathy led them over to a sofa she left them together. "Tom, uh, like Cathy told me it would be good if I talked to you about her Church. See, even though I've only known her a month, I think she's the woman for me, and she says she'd never marry anyone who wasn't a Catholic."

"What's your religious background?" Tom asked Alex, trying to force himself to be friendly.

Finding out that Alex didn't go to the Methodist Church except on Christmas and Easter, Brother Tom recommended he talk to a good priest at the parish nearest his house.

On his way out the door Cathy grabbed Tom by the arm.

"I invited you 'cuz I wanted you to check him out. I figured that we're so close, you would know if he'd be the right one for me, even though he's not Catholic yet."

"I'll pray about it," Brother Tom muttered.

On the way back to the seminary, Tom berated himself for feeling rejected. *After all, she couldn't have chosen me when I'm going for the priesthood.* Besides feeling sad, an old familiar feeling of anxiety started coming up.

He imagined himself cornering Cathy at the hospital and telling her, "I've decided not to be a priest and the reason is I'm so in love with you." Tom felt butterflies in his stomach.

On the way to his room Tom noticed the open door of Father John's room. Not wanting to be seen by his spiritual director without his Franciscan robe on, Tom turned around, went down a flight of stairs and rushed down the corridor to go up the staircase on the opposite end of the hall. Once in his own room Tom hastily undressed and threw his habit over his head and shoulders. Then, taking a deep breath, he walked back slowly up the staircase to Father John's room.

After recounting the embarrassing tale of his uncertainties about the priesthood and his feelings about Cathy, Tom waited nervously to see what Father John would discern.

Coldly, the older priest reminded him of previous advice to avoid getting close to young women during this critical phase of his life as a seminarian. "Go spend an hour before the Blessed Sacrament, Tom, and see if you can renew your promises of celibacy at least for another year. Plenty of time then to decide if God wants you to make your final profession as a Franciscan."

—Analysis of Anxiety—

"I must say a word about fear. It is life's only true opponent. Only fear can defeat life. It is a clever, treacherous adversary…it has no decency, respects no law or convention, shows no mercy. It goes for your weakest spot, which it finds with unerring ease. It begins in your mind, always, one moment you are feeling calm, self-possessed, happy. Then fear, disguised in the garb of mild-mannered doubt, slips in your mind like a spy… Reason comes to do battle for you. You are reassured…but, to your amazement, despite superior tactics and a number of undeniable victories, reason is laid low. You feel yourself weakening, wavering. Your anxiety becomes dread."

Life of Pi by Yann Martel (p. 161)

Anxiety, anxious: dictionary definition—uneasy, apprehensive, worried, disquieted by painful suspense—from the Latin for tormented.

I would add—a feeling of heading toward emotional quicksand.

Fear of rejection is usually accompanied by anxiety. The reason for the fear is often clear. But the anxiety may be a manifestation of deeper insecurities. For example, our heroine Lynn might tell herself that she is afraid that Pete might drop their friendship. But her insecurity may be coming from a much worse thought, such as, "Every attractive man I meet will reject me, and even if I get a Church annulment I will never find a second husband."

Matt knows that he is afraid his son Joey may lose focus during baseball games and fail to be the star he used to be. His overall anxiety, indicated by the revival of the habit of cracking his knuckles, may have a more hidden cause. Will he feel like a failure in his own life if his son stops demonstrating superiority in sports? Will the choice of some other goal by the son be a form of rejection not only of the father's values, but also of their bond?

Even though Brother Tom is not sure he wants to leave the Franciscans, he is still afraid of losing Cathy to another man. The anxiety he feels after meeting Alex, however, might be a deep-seated insecurity about all relationships. What if Father John and the other friars reject him for even considering leaving them?

Whatever the psychological reasons for anxiety, the experience is always painful and disconcerting. We would like to be both exteriorly and interiorly strong, invulnerable…god-like? Anxiety signifies weakness and vulnerability. Philosophers point out that given the reality of death, all human beings are weak and vulnerable. Denying that we could die at any moment for a reason beyond our control, for example, is simply hiding from reality.

In spite of these possible causes for universal anxiety, when we report having anxiety attacks, or simply feeling anxious, we usually mean something more unpleasant and usually more extreme than some primordial sense of being mortal. In the case of anxiety about human relationships, we are usually talking about fear of rejection. For some of us just the knowledge that we cannot control other people is enough to make us feel miserable.

Overcoming fear of rejection will mean, in part, refusing to give others the power to make us feel abandoned. Because we experience God's love, a human's rejection can make us sad. It can wound us, but it doesn't have to make us overly anxious or despairing. How we can move from anxiety about rejection to acceptance and hope will be the subject of later chapters.

For now, let us explore some other facets of anxiety. It is helpful to distinguish between real or only perceived rejection. Real rejection would be when someone tries to get rid of someone else by breaking off the usual forms of contact or by banishing him/her from sight. Remember reading about olden days when disapproving parents of eloping couples wrote letters including such words as "never darken my door again"?

Perceived rejection would be when someone changes the pattern of a relationship not because he or she doesn't care anymore, but for other reasons, sometimes good ones, such as those married-man-Pete is thinking of with regard to Lynn.

Another example. If his son, Joe, opts for art rather than baseball, Matt, and parents like him, may perceive it as rejection, even though it is really just a move toward legitimate independence.

To the extent that Brother Tom allowed fantasies of marriage to Cathy to dominate his imagination, he may have come to regard himself as equally central in her dreams. He will feel rejected if she becomes engaged to another man, even though for Cathy there is no change in her friendly feelings at all.

Typically those anxious about rejection think that some mistake on their part caused the beloved one to cast them out. Could anxiously making amends be a remedy? But usually the reasons for changing the nature of a bond are more complex. Lynn doesn't have to get a new hairdo or become more efficient to maintain her friendship with Pete. She needs to let go of the present mode to adopt a warm but slightly more distant manner. Matt will be able to keep his son's love if he sets him free and affirms him in his new plans. In later chapters we will watch Tom move into a deeper prayer life so that the discernment of his vocation will be less fraught with anxiety about rejection from women or from his spiritual director.

Being somewhat anxious about rejection by friends, spouses, and children is not unusual or contemptibly weak. It is painful, nonetheless, and becomes a red flag if it comes to dominate one's life. For instance, suppose Lynn began to keep her office door open at all times hoping for a glimpse of her boss, or started following him into restaurants to accidentally bump into him or to sit at his table.

Insistence on controlling others beyond what is legitimate also stems from anxiety. If Joe's dad, Matt, were to threaten his son with the loss of driving privileges unless he continued with baseball, that would indicate extreme underlying anxiety.

Trying to break up Cathy's relationship to her new boyfriend, or to win his spiritual director over by public flattery and subservient behavior, would be a symptom in Tom of out of proportion anxiety.

Understanding anxiety about rejection requires knowledge about psychological causes. I am not a professional counselor or psychoanalyst. Just the same, from years of being helped by such healers, I have come to some basic convictions I want to share with you.

Let us look first at childhood anxiety. According to most therapists, even babes in the womb can feel insecure, especially at the moment when they usher forth from the protection of their mother's bodies. Parents of newborns, exhausted by having to tend to the needs of their little ones, may wonder why they cry so much. We are told that not only do infants experience much physical pain from thirst, gases in the stomach, etc., but they also feel abandoned whenever they are separated from the embrace of the parents, especially the mother. Having no sense of time, the loss of the proximity of Mother for even a few minutes can seem endless.

According to Judith Viorst, author of *Necessary Losses: The Loves, Illusions, Dependencies and Impossible Expectations That All of Us Have to Give Up in Order to Grow* (New York: Fawcett, 1986), separation from the mother is the major cause of anxiety in all of us, persisting symbolically over and over again in youth and adulthood.

This quotation from a book about the famous English statesman Disraeli illustrates the need a man might feel for a woman's love in an ambiguous relationship. Disraeli, himself married but unhappily, was in love with a married woman who thought that their friendship must be expressed less. She loved him too, but thought he was wanting more of her time than was right for a man to want of a married woman. He tried to bring her around by saying, "Without love, one does not live. One merely exists in a grey world." *Disraeli: Portrait of a Romantic* (p. 442)

Going back to a psychological perspective, I was interested to reflect on this theory: in order to survive, the child must obey the parents; rejection by them could actually cause death.

In later life, there can be anxiety that refusing to comply can lead to rejection, translated into a visceral, if not fully conscious, fear of annihilation.

"Man is not meant to be alone." The desire to be close in relationship to others is not abnormal, and is, in fact, God-willed. We often describe ourselves in terms of our loved ones. "I am the son or daughter of these parents…the sister or brother of him or her…one of this or that group of friends…the wife or husband of our spouses." For this reason, a part of our very identity is threatened when rejection looms.

Children of divorced parents are said to believe their bad behavior is the cause of the loss of the parent no longer in the home. Since in most cases, divorce results in a lower degree of economic security, children can pick up a sense of threat to their very existence.

When a parent dies leaving children behind, the usual anxiety about separation is greatly increased, sometimes leading to a fear of bonding with anyone, or, sometimes causing a frightened desire to overly-control all loved ones, to keep them safe.

The founder of psychoanalysis, Sigmund Freud, is said to have replied to the question, "What do women want?" with the unexpected answer: "They want to control men!"

Could one find echoes of these phenomena in our stories? Could Pete be attracted to Lynn partly because he finds in her friendship a motherly warmth to counter-balance the tensions in the mainly masculine world of business? Lynn, having separated from her husband, with nearly full-grown sons, might like having a bond with a man who needs her help in his work. The best friend of the boss seems like a secure role. If Pete rejects her, how bleak would be her impersonal work at the furniture store!

Is it an accident that Joe finds it possible to loosen the tight bond with his father partly because he has a girlfriend to give him feminine affirmation? Does Matt need to control his son because he takes his identity from this child: father of the baseball star?

Does Tom feel anxious about his celibate vocation where he would be bonded to Franciscan fathers and brothers, but have to exist without the motherly love of a woman?

A different source of insights about anxiety in relationships comes from the development within the 12 Step Self Help Programs of a specialty called CoDA—short for co-dependency. (See: "About Co-Dependents Anonymous")

Here is one part of the program you might want to use to better understand your own anxieties about rejection:

> "Participants are advised to admit to having tried to use others as our sole source of identity, value and well-being, and as a way of trying to restore within us the emotional losses from our childhoods and of having linked their dreams for the future to the other person with fear of being hurt and rejected."

The twelve promises co-dependent members make include these:

- To believe that feelings of emptiness and loneliness will disappear, leading to a new sense of belonging.
- Not to be controlled by one's fears. Overcome fear and act with courage, integrity, and dignity.
- To release from worry, guilt and regret about my past and present. Not to repeat destructive patterns.
- Develop and maintain healthy and loving relationships. Most helpful, I found was this paragraph:

"The need to control and manipulate others will disappear as I learn to trust those who are trustworthy... I no longer need to rely solely on others to provide my sense of worth. I gradually experience serenity, strength, and spiritual growth in my daily life."

More about how to move into this greater serenity will be found in future chapters.

Here is an insightful passage about fear from a Catholic treatise by Father Raniero Cantalamessa:

"Have No Fear! The Gospel's dominant theme this Sunday is that Christ frees us from fear...dangerous are chronic fears, those that live with us, which we carry from our birth or childhood, which become part of our being, and which sometimes we end up being attached to... Anxiety has become the illness of the century... The anxious person suffers evils twice over: first in the anticipation and then in the reality.

"...The remedy is summarized in one word: to trust God, to believe in Providence and in the heavenly Father's love. The real root of all fears is that of finding oneself alone, like that continuous fear of the child of being abandoned. And Jesus assures us precisely about this: that we will not be abandoned. 'For my father and my mother have forsaken me, but the Lord will take me up,' says Psalm (27:10).

"Even if all were to abandon us, the Lord would not. His love is stronger than all... (Jesus) himself wished to live this experience. It is written that, in the Garden of Olives 'he began to feel sadness and anxiety.' The original text even suggests the idea of a solitary terror, as of someone who feels removed from human association, in an immense solitude..."

Notice in this closing passage from Scripture how fear is linked to trusting too much in human love instead of trusting in the love of the Lord:

"Cursed be the man that trusts in man...whose heart departs from the Lord. For he shall be like the heath in the desert and shall not see when good comes; but shall inhabit the parched places in the wilderness, in a salt land not inhabited. Blessed is the man that trusts in the Lord and whose hope is in the Lord. For he shall be as a tree planted by the waters that spreads out its roots by the river and shall not see when heat comes, but her leaf shall be green...and shall not cease from yielding fruit." (Jeremiah 17:5-8)

REJECTION

Pete never talked to Lynn about his strategy of taking her to lunch only occasionally instead of every week. He had the feeling she understood that he didn't want to hurt his marriage by getting too close to another woman.

But one Monday Lynn rushed into Pete's office begging for advice on how to deal with her wayward teenage son. The conversation spilled over into lunch hour. "I wish you could talk to him, Pete," Lynn sighed. "It's tough with his father being such a low-life."

Remembering his own youthful sins and the terrible guilt when a girlfriend admitted to having an abortion, Pete said he could come over to Lynn's house one evening to try to help her son sort out his morals. Pete's wife, Joy, knew about the plan and promised to pray for the outcome.

When Pete came home at 11 PM, however, Joy was waiting up. In a gentle voice, she said, "Look, honey, I know you have a heart of gold and only want to save this kid, but I think you're playing with fire. Sounds to me as if this woman is in love with you... Use me as an excuse. Just tell her your wife is very jealous and you have to cut out seeing her outside the store."

The next day Pete came into Lynn's office and closed the door behind him. With an unusually serious look on his face, the handsome man made it short, "Lynn, I hope you know I really appreciate all the help you give me, and I really care about you and your sons, but my wife doesn't understand. I'm going to have to stop seeing you except professionally. I promise to pray for you and the family."

Tears came into Lynn's eyes. "Of course, Pete. I understand. It's fine. God bless you." With that, she abruptly got up and went to the ladies' room. Once alone, Lynn put her arms around herself and swayed back and forth. She felt terrible pain in her whole body. Pulling herself together, Lynn got through the day. Driving home she decided she should quit her job. The idea of having to pretend that Pete was only her boss and meant nothing to her seemed unendurable.

Not wanting her son to see the tears in case he was home, Lynn stopped first at the parish. Sitting in a pew in the adoration chapel, she asked God, "Why is life so tough? I've just about gotten over my awful marriage and now this. How do you expect me to make it without real friends even?"

On Lynn's way out of Church she noticed a sign on the bulletin board about a 12 Step Co-dependency group meeting nearby. There was a list of questions to lure people to come. One was, "Do you overreact when relationships break up?" Lynn stared at the question. *Overreact? Is that what I'm doing?*

Matt and Joey

Matt grabbed the envelope sitting on Joe's plate with the return address: Admissions Boston College.

Carol took the roast out of the oven and laid it down on the trivet. "Hey, Matt, that's for Joey. Why are you reading it?"

Matt grunted and continued reading the letter. "Scholarship for five thousand dollars a year. That's good." Then he banged his fist on the table. "What the hell? The scholarship is from the Art Department!"

Carol intoned grace. "Bless us, O Lord and—"

Matt interrupted. "He's not taking it. The baseball scholarship offers should be here by next week."

When Joe came in late for dinner his father confronted him right away. "Joey, my son, so you applied for an art scholarship even though I told you to stick with baseball?"

Joe tried not to look into his father's eyes. He looked at

the letter from Boston College and then cut off a big piece of beef and chewed it slowly. Then remembering to say grace he made the sign of the cross hurriedly.

"I guess I can't put it off any longer, Dad. I know how much you've always dreamed I'd be a baseball star but, frankly, I just got tired of it. I know I can be an artist and that's what I really want to do, so I'd appreciate it if you would stop pressuring me about a career in sports."

Matt glared at his son. The father never brought up the topic of college again. He stopped going to the last baseball games of the high school season, and conversed with his son only about practical matters such as the use of the car.

Carol expected her husband to be upset about Joey's decision, but not to such a degree. The first sign was that Matt stopped watching TV with Carol in the evening. Instead he shut himself up in their bedroom and played interactive games on the computer.

Within a few more months Matt omitted their usual love-making on Saturday nights. Looking at her nice figure in the long mirror each day she would think to herself, *Carol, old gal, you still seem pretty spiffy for a forty-year-old—no grey in the strawberry-blond hair, no middle-age spread, 130 lbs. Must be him not me.*

One night, just before turning out the light, Carol decided to check it out. "Matt, sweetheart, what's going on? Have I become a leper?"

"Just leave me alone, babe," Matt replied. "It's not the military. I don't have to perform on schedule."

Alarmed that Matt might be getting into some sort of post-mid-life 50s crisis, Carol decided to consult Joe's best friend from their parish Knights of Columbus chapter.

Tom and Cathy

It was ten months after the party where Cathy had introduced Tom to her boyfriend, Alex. Dutifully, Tom arranged that the man whom he thought of secretly as his rival, would join the Rite of Christian Initiation classes to eventually become confirmed as a Catholic.

He was glad there was no occasion to have to see cute red-headed Cathy with Alex since he only saw her at the hospital where he still went to minister once a week. In spite of all his prayers, he couldn't seem to root out the pain of feeling rejected even though Cathy was still such a good friend, and the envy he felt whenever he contrasted good-looking, tall Alex with his own short, stocky, unattractive self.

One afternoon during their usual now-only-weekly coffee break at the hospital cafeteria, Cathy was beaming. She lifted the back of her hand right in Tom's face to show off her engagement ring. The seminarian forced a smile of congratulations, and after a few perfunctory questions about the date of the wedding made an excuse to leave the table.

Back at the Franciscan seminary, Tom made an appointment for that evening to see his spiritual director, Fr. John. Face to face sitting in their brown robes on wooden chairs, Tom asked, "If I feel so miserable about Cathy's wedding, doesn't that prove that I have a married vocation, after all? I mean, why would I feel so rejected when I didn't even make a play for her?"

Fr. John joined his hands as if in prayer and raised them to his lips, closing his eyes for a few minutes of silent cogitation. "Feeling jealous of a man who will marry the girl you're in love with is not unusual for any man, Tom. Remember St. Francis throwing himself into a thorn-bush in agony about having given up marriage and children?"

Tom squirmed in his seat. "Okay. Does that mean that everyone who admires St. Francis is called to be a celibate religious?"

"You want me to tell you what to do, Tom. That's kind of old Church. Nowadays we think that novices need to be absolutely sure in their own hearts that God is calling them... not be able to say later, 'I felt pressured by the Order.' To tell you the truth, my theory is that when God doesn't give a clear sign for the religious life, it is often because the candidate would then be guilty if he refused...like God puts you on a long leash to see what your will is. A vocation is an invitation, not a prison sentence!"

Tom frowned. "So, in the meantime, what should I do

with these terrible feelings…when what I really feel like doing is jumping off a bridge?"

If Fr. John felt compassion for his directee, he didn't show it. Instead, he stood up and walked around the small parlor adjoining his bedroom, and without sitting down again suggested, "I'm going to make an appointment for you with Dr. Greg."

"Who's he?"

"He's a Catholic counselor who offers free consultations to our men. Look, Tom, we had you pegged as the man most likely to persevere with your fervent prayer life and love of serving the needy. I have a feeling you have to get to the root of your anxiety about rejection before you can make any big decisions."

—Analysis of Rejection—

"So Jacob went in to Rachel also, and he loved Rachel more than Leah… When the Lord saw that Leah was hated, he opened her womb; but Rachel was barren." (Genesis 29:30-31)

There may be worse things than rejection. I imagine such horrors as awaiting death by guillotine. The death of my son by suicide was certainly more heartbreaking than the worst rejection. Still, in terms of the acuteness of the pain, surely rejection is among the most devastating.

My description of a process gone through by many victims of rejection may fit your own experience only in part. Read the rest of this chapter even if you don't identify with the first part. What does not fit your case, will help you understand the sufferings of others, including those you reject!

With myself in the past, and others I have known well, I see a pattern of reacting to rejection with suicidal despair; bitterness; hope against hope; finally hitting bottom in a dull sense of insuperable misery.

Even if you have never tried to commit suicide because of the pain of rejection, attempted it, or threatened to do so, feeling like, "I'll die if he/she leaves me," or "Life isn't worth living if…" signify that somehow you have given power to another person to make the continuance of your life worthwhile.

Even people who believe that God loves them, or who "strut their stuff" as if they thought they were the most wonderful people in the world, may still feel desperate from rejection. Lynn and Tom both think that without the love of Pete or Cathy their lives will be almost unbearable. Matt thinks that without his son's obedience to his wishes, he is nothing.

Tom, the seminarian, could have written the words himself of the fictional character in the quotation below:

"I feel worthless. My whole life's been justified by
the belief that Elizabeth genuinely cared about me

and that I was wonderful. I ought to have known right from the start that this belief was nothing but a grand illusion. I'm not worth caring about, never was. I'm useless, a failure, a total waste of space... better to jump into the black pit right now and make an end of it. Then I won't need anything anymore, least of all love... I hate myself for not being good enough for her to love me."

From Susan Howatch, *The Heartbreaker*
(pp. 336-337)

In his poem, "Lovesong," Ted Hughes describes the ecstatic sexual union he enjoyed with his wife. In spite of this joy, he left his lover-bride, Sylvia Plath, also a poet. She committed suicide eighteen months after the break up, even though they had little children.

"He loved her and she loved him
His kisses sucked out her whole past and future or
tried to
He had no other appetite
She bit him she gnawed him she sucked
She wanted him complete inside her
Safe and sure forever and ever
Their little cries fluttered into the curtains...

He gripped her hard so that life
Should not drag her from that moment
He wanted all future to cease
He wanted to topple with his arms round her
Off that moment's brink and into nothing
Or everlasting or whatever there was...
His smiles were the garrets of a fairy palace
Where the real world would never come...
Her love-tricks were the grinding of locks...

In their entwined sleep they exchanged arms and legs
In their dreams their brains took each other hostage

In the morning they wore each other's face"

Collected Poems (p. 255)

With time suicidal despair usually yields to a feeling of bitterness. Why? Why? Why? My son was so perfect, my boss was so perfect, my friend was so perfect, our hearts beat as one...

The following reflections will not be about parental co-dependency relationships, but about the even more common problems of unrequited romantic love.

The sufferings of rejection in such cases is the sense that surrounding spectators consider the rejected ones to have been idiots in the first place to have been so romantic and idealistic. In fact, some students of the human scene blame our tendency in our times to live in illusions to be the result of the 19th century Romantic movement and its offspring, 20th century Hollywood musicals always with happy endings. In so far as romantic poetry, fiction and film gave the impression that total happiness in relationships was waiting around the corner, it set people up for bitter disappointment. Pouring ourselves exclusively into "the impossible dream" has to lead to disillusion, often because of rejection. But even without rejection, a cynic opined that the only remedy for infatuation is marriage!

An old English novel by Claire Davis has this crude fellow say that women pretend to be interested in a man but all they really want is "man's blood and his heart out of his body and his soul and his pride and after she's got him and he's trapped by his longing for her, she wants to eat him up. He has to defend himself by eating her up instead."

How's that for bitterness!

And how about this estimate of love by Napoleon whose adored wife was unfaithful:

> "I have no time to be bothered with feelings and to repent of them like other men… There are two motives of action: self-interest and fear. Believe me, love is a foolish blindness!… I love no one, not even my brothers… Let us leave sensibilities to women. Men should be firm of heart and strong of will, or else they should

have nothing to do with war or governance…. A man
of fifty has done with love… I have an iron heart…"

Napoleon by Emil Ludwig (p. 596)

In our final chapter we will see how healing of rejection
with the help of God's love can open us to the type of relationship that is neither ecstatic nor fatal, but instead realistic,
gentle, tender, and humorous.

Some of us, though bitter over rejection, won't give up. We
hope against hope that the beloved will change, or we repeat the
cycle with fantasies of another perfect person to fill the gap.

Here is a fictional account of the feelings of a young
woman who was seduced by an intellectual rake. He still writes
to her from elsewhere in romantic tones but he didn't return her
desire for a commitment:

"Her mind darkened with the thought that she had
been deceived and that he deceived her, and then
consoled herself with something that she herself
did not understand and which was less likely than
a miracle. 'It is not possible to understand him,' she
thought to herself, 'he is strange and cold, selfish,
moody and capricious, but perhaps all exceptional
men are like that.' In any event what she felt was
more like suffering than love. Her inner flinching

and the break that she felt in the depths of her being made it seem to her that the whole burden of that love which he had provoked lay upon her alone, and that he was lost somewhere far in the fog and the distance which she dared not call by its real name. For a woman in love, even when she has lost all her illusions, cherishes her love like a child she has not been destined to bear."

Ivo Andric, *The Bridge on the Drina* (p. 274)

It is likely that a woman who reacts to rejection with this kind of analysis, will repeat the same pattern with another hero.

Feelings of rejection are universal. Here is a Hispanic explanation, making use of an amusing analogy of the habits of vanilla plants:

"Vanilla, like a woman, needs to have a tree or a strong stalk to twine around and hold it up so it won't die.

"I am so far from being a woman of deep peace. I'm like a dog groveling down with tail wagging, begging for a Scooby treat. And ready to jump at a touch." (p. 54)

The same author, Christina Rivera-Garza, describing rejection from a man's point of view, writes that,

"Men who yearn for a woman consume more energy in the act than in anything else that they do all day. Their faces look exhausted, the muscles that have to bear the weight of the ball and chain, the shackles on their ankles, are permanently tense…all of this will be over only in the parenthesis of morphine." (pp. 208-209)

When the woman this man loves leaves, the man is described this way: "Pride prevents him from crying. The absurd nakedness of a sentimental man embarrasses him." (p. 220)

Christina Rivera-Garza, *No One Will See Me Cry*

Let me speak for myself. Up until fairly recently, in spite of many painful experiences of rejection, after which I fled to the love of Jesus to let Him lick my wounds, I would always try again on the same unrealistic basis. How well I understood this line from the old classic Lorna Doone, "Despair is hope just dropped asleep for better chance of dreaming." (p. 529)

The last time round, I got a healing image: I can't just go running around with a begging bowl measuring how much love I can get from this one or that one. Better to let Jesus fill the begging bowl of love so that everything else is just gravy.

Sometimes those who are divorced and re-married several

times feel rejected during each attempt. They then look for the perfect spouse who will never reject them and whom they will never reject. This can come from a false idea that happiness is attainable on earth. A friend of mine once wrote me this about divorce in relation to romantic ideals of happiness:

"The concept of 'happiness' keeps coming to mind. Popular American culture from Gershwin to the soaps keys people into the notion that personal happiness is the paramount aim in life to be distinguished from living a useful, productive life, living a life centered on what one was created to do, etc. Happiness in the modern sense is focused on the idea that another person can 'save' me, that another person can provide the basis for my own personal fulfillment, that a relationship with a fated one (the ideal) will solve the problem of my life and place me in a new life condition of happiness and fulfillment. (i.e. through him or her, I will finally get what I really want)…

"But my experience is that happiness does not work that way. First of all, people can't save each other. What they can do, and this is beyond price, is to help each other (the biblical 'helpmate.') How long it takes to realize that friends, not lovers, are the best things in life! And to have the possibility of both in their due and deepening seasons, as committed husbands and wives can...

"Secondly, happiness is not a permanent or stable condition; it is a sense of well-being and beatitude, and, this side of the world to come, it is (in my experience, and by its very nature) partial and elusive (there on Tuesday, overwhelmed by events on Wednesday; glimpsed in a recalled memory or on a stroll; or in the satisfaction of some accomplishment, or in the delight of a beloved); but elusive, a perception, a gift, a 'find,' not a possession, not a state of affairs."

What makes some of us hit bottom on rejection? The pain? The lost hope of healing? It is hard to say, but what is clear is that for many of us the only reason for seeking a remedy is an awful bleak unendurable suffering that makes us grab any remedy we can find.

Of course, there are remedies which are not remedies, such as indulgence in addictions to alcohol or drugs. Such problems require specific treatment such as 12 Step Programs, rehabilitation, counseling, best combined with the type of spiritual surrender to God that will be the theme of our next chapter.

It was hard to write this description and analysis of rejection. Probably it was hard to read it. Dwelling on the sufferings of rejection unrelieved by all the other aspects of life cushioning the pain, is itself very, very, hard. I thought it necessary to describe the worst so that you will believe me when I write about how surrender to God can really heal. Would you believe me, and the other witnesses who will write about their salvation from human rejection, if you thought your experience was worse?

May this last quotation be a hint of healing possibilities:

"He will leave you at once and give His favors to others if you play Him false with anyone, trying to please anyone more than Him." (p. 98)

"Adulterous desires press in upon the heart where the footprints of the spouse are still plain to be seen... Never let this happen to us, Lord, and even if we do so fall away through human frailty, never let us despair on that account, but let us hasten back to the merciful healer who lifts up the helpless ones out of the dust...for He who never desires the death of a sinner will tend us and heal us again and again."

Guigo II, *The Ladder of Monks*, pp. 91-92

SURRENDER

Three months after Pete quit having a weekly luncheon with Lynn, she dropped by his office, face glowing.

"Can you take a break? I want to tell you about how well my CoDA group is going—this great group I started attending."

Pete looked puzzled.

"CoDA is short for Co-dependency Anonymous."

Pete buzzed his secretary and told her to tell any callers he was in a meeting.

"I'm all ears. I've been praying for you, Lynn. Hoping for good things in your life after all the suffering you had with your husband."

Lynn began to describe the co-dependency group. "You wouldn't believe what a difference it makes that we don't give each other advice but just follow the program! It says in the manual that without cross-talk people feel free to share without worrying about judgment and ridicule."

"Hey, back up. I don't even know what co-dependency is."

Lynn blushed. "Well, kinda like you know how sometimes a lot of us kinda cling to someone else as if they could save us, when it's not realistic or appropriate. You could even be co-dependent on a spouse. That's what I'm learning. It's not unusual for women like me to stay with an abusive alcoholic husband for years before separating. It's because we're weak. We think we can't stand on our own feet. Well, we can't, of course. We need God." Lynn opened up her little CoDA handbook. Listen to this: "We can experience a new freedom from our self-defeating lifestyles…free from the emotional bonds of our past and compulsive control of our present…to be that which God intended—precious and free." (p. 5)

"I thought you were a strong Catholic. Didn't you lean on God before?" Pete asked.

"Yes and no. Not in the Twelve Step sense, where you admit, 'My life is out of control. Without you, God, I'm not going to make it.' In the group we are taught how to trust God to give us what we need. I've started going to the Adoration chapel after work each day to 'let go, let God' as they say in CoDA."

"Really? My wife insists on her adoration hour each night after she puts the kids to bed. I miss her sitting next to me watching TV, but it seems to give her the strength to get through the day better."

Pete glanced at his watch. "I should let the phone calls come in soon, Lynn, but before you go, I've been wondering if there are other changes you need to make in your lifestyle?"

Lynn winked. "Well, don't mention it to anyone else here, but one of the things I probably have to change is working here. Accounting brings in good money, but as a separated woman with grown children, I probably need a much more person-to-person kind of job. I'm thinking maybe of selling the big house, living more simply, working for Catholic Charities, and maybe slowly getting a degree in counseling in the evening."

"Sounds great to me, Lynn, even though we'd all miss ya much."

Surrendering to God about relationships with men didn't mean that Lynn shed tendencies to look for ideal men, but it was a bridge to eventually being more realistic and less devastated when things didn't work out.

Matt and Joey

When Matt's wife, Carol, saw that her husband's depression was not going to go away, she had a long talk with Craig, the friend she thought Joe admired the most. Craig was a man fifteen years older than Matt, now in his sixties, who ran the Knights of Columbus chapter at their parish.

"Sure, I'll talk to him, Carol. It could take a while. Mid-life hits many men pretty hard, some at forty but others at fifty, even if they don't have such a disappointment with a son."

After the next meeting of the Knights, Craig asked Matt if he would go out with him for a burger. "Had to work overtime and missed dinner," he gave as the reason. Matt hesitated but then agreed.

"So, how's life treating you, old pal?" Craig opened.

Matt looked around to see if anyone at one of the Burger King tables knew him. He lowered his voice, just in case. Carol had many friends he wouldn't recognize.

"To tell you the truth, Craig, I'm about the lowest I've ever been. The job is so routine I could repair phones in my sleep. Carol's a great wife and all, but you know, after so many years it's not exactly exciting to be with her day or night—pretty predictable. With Joey dropping out of baseball and Dee hardly ever at home…what do I have to look forward to?"

"Know what you mean. When my Zach left for a university all the way across the country in California, it was like all the pizzazz went out of my life. I even began to doubt God. I was getting so glum my wife forced me to talk to Fr. Murphy."

"Yeah? I'm surprised. You always seem pretty up-beat to me, Craig. Like every man would like to be at your age."

Craig put down the remains of his burger and looked at Matt eyeball to eyeball as he continued his story. "Fr. Murphy told me to say a special prayer to St. Joseph every night before going to bed. I'll try to find it for you. It went something like this:

"St. Joseph, you had many problems in your life. Help me to trust that God will show me what to do. The angels helped you make decisions. Let me not rely on my own mind, but to be open to new paths God might want me to travel on."

After ordering a slice of apple pie, Craig continued telling Matt about what happened. "I was skeptical, but after saying that prayer a few months every night, I began to see that I might need to make some changes in my plans for the future. That was when I left my dull but well-paying job selling insurance and started teaching business classes at the Junior College, mostly to disadvantaged students. Never regretted it."

Matt ordered a slice of pie to prolong the encounter. Craig moved into the parish when he was already teaching and Matt hadn't heard much about the transition. "So, do you think I might need a change, too?"

"Why don't you write your own prayer to St. Joseph and see what happens? Maybe something unexpected will open up."

"By the way," Craig added, "around this time my wife persuaded me to go to daily Mass for Lent. At first I thought it was too much to get up an hour earlier for the seven-thirty

Mass before leaving for work. But after awhile I found I had a lot more peace. When Lent was over I kept up the practice."

When Matt summarized the conversation for Carol that night, she looked hopeful. Trying not to pressure him so that he wouldn't resist her, she shared, "You know, Matt, if you wanted to take a job that would be more interesting but it paid less, I'm dying to go back to work."

Matt wrote his own prayer to St. Joseph. "St. Joe, you surrendered totally to God even though the future was not clear. Help me to surrender and to want to do His will, no matter what."

A few months later Matt was offered a low-paying job—but one with benefits—as assistant sports' coach at the high school where Joey used to be a star. Pretty soon he began to enjoy helping and encouraging the guys and gals on the teams, even when they were not star players. In thanksgiving for his new life, Matt started going with Carol to Mass on Friday mornings as well as the obligatory Sunday liturgy.

When Joey came home for vacations, the relationship was still a little strained. Joey made a point of attending some of the games his father was coaching and planned eventually to get his dad more into the appreciation of art.

Tom and Cathy

Weekly sessions with Dr. Greg, the counselor Fr. John had recommended, were tougher than the young man had imagined, even though the rapport was good from the beginning. Tom immediately liked the round, bearded older man. He found Dr. Greg much easier to talk to than his spiritual director. *I guess because he's an authority figure*, Tom realized as more and more came out about how the seminarian's relationship to the older Franciscans in charge resembled his difficulties as a kid with his father.

That was one of the first revelations. "I thought we'd mostly be talking about my infatuation with Cathy. How come you change the subject whenever I bring her up?" he had asked Dr. Greg after the first month of counseling.

"Cathy is what we call the 'presenting problem,' but my guess has been from the start that your closeness to her near the time of making first vows in the community is because you are afraid of having to live without feminine love if you become a Franciscan."

Probing made it clear that Tom's dependence on his mother had been one of the factors that distanced his father from him. Tom's mother loved to cook and beamed at her large family as she served them seconds. Her only son, Tom, the youngest, turned out to be the one most overweight, the butt of ridicule at school. His father, one of those lean wired men who can eat huge amounts of food without gaining weight, came to despise his son for his gluttony.

Tom's mother was a daily communicant. When the boy was little she took him with her to Mass at the Franciscan Church. This was when Tom began to love the liturgy and dream of one day being a priest.

After many months of more casual conversation about Tom's reactions to the other Franciscans, especially his teachers and mentors, Dr. Greg offered to pray for a healing of memories for Tom. He had Tom lie down on the sofa. After running through some of the standard evocations of past life from womb to youth, Dr. Greg raised his voice slightly and insisted, "Now I want you to try to remember the very worst moment you ever had with your Dad."

It took a while, but then the burly young adult began to sob and then the words to describe that experience came out slowly. "We all took turns going fishing with Dad... The older girls had their Sunday afternoons with him and I was next... I had the day marked on my calendar with a big red circle... I guess I was about thirteen. After Sunday lunch Dad started out the door toward the garage where the fishing gear was kept. I followed him out. He turned around and stared at me coldly. 'Forget it, son. With all you shoveled in at dinner today you might tip over the boat.'"

"Tell me what it felt like, Tom."

More tears. "I guess I just felt totally rejected…that nothing I would ever do would please him because I would never be like him."

At the visit a week after, Dr. Greg asked Tom to describe echoes of that great father-rejection pain in later life. Over time the seminarian came to see that he had a pattern of trying to get close to the colder men in any situation such as school or the parish, brushing aside as insignificant friendship offered him by warmer mentor figures. He would rationalize, "Those guys love me because they love everyone," instead of allowing the affirmation of such men to raise his self-esteem.

Talking to Cathy, still his best friend even though she was married now, he was able to explain, "You know Dr. Greg is terrific. I'll be sorry when I have to leave. One of his best insights was that I secretly think God the Father is cold. Fr. John, my spiritual director, says that when I can open myself to experience God's truly fatherly love for me, I'll be better able to discern if I have a vocation. I'll be able to trust that if I am called to be a priest He will give me all the human love I need as well."

—Analysis of Surrender—

"If goodness lead him not,
yet weariness may toss him to My breast."

George Herbert

Of those who feel rejected many will not make it to the surrender to God that will help them the most. A reason can be that we can get stuck dwelling on the wrongs done by the rejecting persons.

When Pete told Lynn that he couldn't see her anymore outside the store, in her feelings of hurt Lynn could have tried to fight back. She might have insisted that his wife was wrong about their friendship being dangerous and, therefore, Pete was wrong to drop her as a friend. If he refused to resume the previous mode of their relationship, she could retaliate by talking badly about him to the other employees at the store, or quitting in a huff but replaying the drama of her rejection over and over again in her head.

If Matt had not consulted his wise older friend Craig about his crisis, he might have continued on in bitterness and a kind of sour grapes rejection of his son and wife.

On a rebound, Tom might have taken up with a hidden substitute girlfriend, meanwhile pursuing the priesthood with the Franciscans but forming a faction in the Order of disobedient brothers.

Even if we ourselves have indulged in some of the negative modes of dealing with rejection described above, most of those reading this book will be also looking for a more positive Godly solution.

After rejection we feel crushed. If we do not succumb to

despair, slowly hope begins to emerge out of our very sense of powerlessness. An experience of mine illustrates this experience: a man I loved very much, in a codependent manner, told me that he was in love with another woman. I felt devastated. Because this man was extremely good-looking in a spiritual way, his rejection made me feel ugly. As I was falling into a pit of despair, Jesus seemed to catch me up in His arms. He seemed to say, "The way you feel rejected by this man is the way I feel rejected by you!"

I was stunned. I don't reject Jesus. I go to daily Mass to let Him teach me and to receive Him into my body and soul and pray in many other ways throughout the day. So how could I be rejecting Him, I wondered. As He spoke in my heart I realized that He was talking about something still deeper. "Aren't I beautiful enough for you? Why do you turn away from Me to grab onto human idols when I alone can give you the love you need?"

After surrendering to Christ in the very place of my bloodied heart, even though there was residual anguish about the man who rejected me, I was gradually able to let go of him and cling tighter to my Savior. It felt as if before I was holding His hand with one of mine, but the other was clutching the hand of my friend. Now both of my hands were in those of Jesus.

Afterwards, even though, in my weakness, I tried over and over again to draw "perfect" people to me, I somehow knew deep down that Jesus would always be there for me to return to. The time it took to let go of others got shorter.

Here is another image I had years later at another time of rejection:

Does one who is totally vulnerable become invulnerable (because there is no pride left to squash?)

As under the heavy tread of the giant tire, the tiniest of the ants escapes from the hill?

The strutting tyrant, the bravado tongue one day becomes a handful of dust while the "tiny" soul soars into Light?

God became a babe!
The second person of the Trinity a circle of bread!
While the rustic maid becomes the Queen of heaven!

If everyone is seen as but a poor little thing even I, I, i, will the kingdom come?

A mentor of mine, the lay contemplative, Charles Rich, wrote,

"How sad it is to think that the hearts made for love fail to turn to the only source which can fill up the need for that love. It is to Christ we must have re-course if we wish to be genuinely happy and to Him only… How disappointing creatures are when con-trasted with the good Jesus is! How pathetic is the effort men make to fill up their hearts with all that Christ is not and how frustrating and disappointing such efforts are."

As we will see in the chapter about real love, it is not that God wants us exclusively for Himself, without any human love. He does want us to enjoy the love He, Himself, puts in the hearts of others for us. But He knows that unless we seek first the kingdom of heaven, our human loves will become distorted and hurtful. As one writer put it:

> "If in marriage it is three who make a union—the bride, the groom, and the Creator—then it must be so for friendship also. Friend or lover, by the gates of your heart there must stand a watchman, and that watchman is Truth. If you ignore his warnings, you must surely know that you are choosing. You alone are responsible for what must come to pass: the death of Love."
>
> Michael D. O'Brien, *Father Elijah*, (p. 365)

Only God can heal the rejected heart. My words and the

words of other writers I will quote in the rest of this analysis are not exact descriptions of how He can help you, but rather pointers so that you will want to pray to be open to and receptive of His love in whatever way He will choose to give it to you.

Surrender to God after rejection presupposes, of course, that there is actually a God of love who is personally beckoning us to come closer. A contemplative hermit, Brother Thomas of Catholic Solitudes, once suggested I might entitle this chapter "The Divine Longing for the Human Heart." I love those words. They encapsulate the spirituality of the Sacred Heart. There was a time in the Church around the 17th century when many Catholics thought of God almost exclusively as the Almighty, Lord, with His love rarely spoken of. Jesus had always revealed Himself to His friends as infinite personal love, but many in that era had lost the sense of this friendship. To counteract the tendency to over-emphasize fear of God over His love, Jesus appeared to St. Mary Margaret Alacoque in many visions. He pointed to His Sacred Heart. He wanted her to inform His children how rejected He felt because we stayed far from Him. He tried to explain through messages to her and to other contemplatives that He longed for our love.

Just as when we are in love we want to flood the beloved one with all the affection of our hearts, so does God want to engulf us, but we scarcely care as we busily pursue our own agendas!

Maybe you have doubts. Maybe you are thinking, *If*

God showed me His love the way that is being described here, I would be happy. No rejection of any lesser person would bother me.

All I can say is that those who have surrendered to His love in faith and who give themselves time every day to be in His presence, do experience exquisite moments of divine love, or at least much greater peace, security and strength. At the end of this chapter I will provide a meditation to help you enter into the experience of God's love, if you have not already done so.

That human love, even when there is no rejection, is not enough to give us total happiness is no new idea in the spirituality of the Church. St. Augustine proclaimed that "our hearts are restless until they rest in Thee." Pascal wrote of a God-sized vacuum in our souls that only God can fill. In the Old Testament this truth was expressed in the image of the jealous God who will not let us choose anyone over Himself. The first commandment is to love God above all.

Here are a few more vivid expressions of the need to replace disordered illusions with surrender to God:

"Love is the unfamiliar Name
Behind the hands that wove
The intolerable shirt of flame
Which human power cannot remove.

We only

live, only suspire

consumed by either fire or fire."

from T.S. Eliot "Four Quartets"

For a more contemporary expression of the same idea—

"Anything can become an idol...a nation, a political party—drink, drugs, food, football, rock music, pop stars, cards, boats, designer clothes, sex, exercise, loads of money—you name it. All these things may be good in themselves, but once they become an obsession you squander time and energy on illusions, your priorities get rearranged, your balanced lifestyle goes down the tubes and your true self gets stomped on or, in other words, getting cut off from reality can make you psychologically, mentally, and spiritually ill...line yourself up with Ultimate Reality...and you become real in your turn, playing your part in the scheme of things—feeling fulfilled as your real self has the chance to flourish."

Susan Howatch, The Heartbreaker (p. 340)

Infatuation is "desires, hesitancy, whimsy, excitement, bashfulness, bold parry, pleasure...not as big as what the heart yearns for." Julianne Loesch Wiley, *Emma* (p. 123)

Contemplatives often capture in beautiful language what God is ready to give to those who surrender to Him after trying to grab onto human persons only to be rejected. For instance, a man who had felt unloved as a child realized in one huge mystical experience of God when he was in his forties that all the time he had regretted not being loved, he had been in the sea of God's love.

Here is a beautiful contemplative poem from Hannah Hurnard's book, *Mountains of Spices*.

Can love be terrible, my Lord?
Can gentleness be stern?
Ah yes!—intense is love's desire
To purify his loved—'tis fire,
A holy fire to burn.
For he must fully perfect thee

Till in thy likeness all may see
The beauty of thy Lord.

Can holy love be jealous, Lord?
Yes, jealous as the grave;
Till every hurtful idol be
Uptorn and wrested out of thee
Love will be stern to save;
Will spare thee not a single pain

Till thou be freed and pure again
And perfect as thy Lord.

Can love seem cruel, O my Lord?
Yes, like a sword the cure;
He will not spare thee, sin-sick soul,
Till he hath made thy sickness whole,
Until thy heart is pure.
For oh! He loves thee far too well
To leave thee in thy self-made hell,
A Savior is thy Lord!

Gabrielle Bossis was a French actress who devoted her art to presenting Catholic themes on the stage. Jesus spoke in her heart and His words became part of a journal eventually published under the name of *He and I*. As you read these words why not insert your own name—as in putting "Ronda" before the first sentence below: Ronda, why...

> "Why should I who am Love itself, not have my moments of mysterious, secret love, a love of my own choosing?" (p. 65)

> "Forget yourself and remember me—not as an exacting tyrant but a Lamb slain for love." (p. 88)

"Take the place of John and Mary Magdalene. And at the same time be yourself, you, whom I wanted in this century, this period, this little moment of time on earth, my poor little bride." (p. 154)

"I am the Ravisher. Don't struggle. And because you let yourself be taken captive, I'll bring you into my secret garden among the flowers and fruit. You will wear that wedding ring on your finger and we will talk together. In love everything is simple.

"Stretch out your two empty hands to Me. Give Me a big place in your life. Give Me all of it." (p. 161)

"Even on earth you prefer to love a superior person, don't you? Aren't you attracted by intelligence? Warmth? Kindness? Multiply by infinity all the gifts that you look for in those you love, God is more… and this very God wants to possess you." (p. 175)

Here is a meditation on the Song of Songs written by Charles Rich, a lay contemplative:

"More delightful is your love than wine. What beauty, what goodness, truth, joy, pleasantness and delight can for one instant be compared with God's own, substantial, and infinite Beauty? Who…can be compared with Christ?... God became man so that we can have someone whom we can love without any reservation and to an unlimited degree. There is nothing God has made to which we can yield up our whole heart and our whole mind, for nothing exists which warrants such a complete surrender. Only God alone can be loved unconditionally."

Once Jesus seemed to send me this message:

"I want to draw you close in against My heart. I desire unity with you, dearest, but you pull away because you do not trust your Jesus. Would I ever fail you? Would I ever send you a plan that was detrimental to your spirituality and your unity with Me? You know that I would not because My desire, like your desire, is unity.

"I want to draw you directly into My heart, and I want to do that now. You need do nothing, only trust. Tell Me you trust Me all through each day. You desire My happiness and you seek to comfort Me. I will be comforted by unity with you. That is what your Savior desires. Ask Me to give you heightened trust. Practice trusting Me. Ask yourself, what would I decide to do right now if I totally trusted Jesus?

The answers will come to you and you will struggle less with doubts and anxieties. These things are not from Me and they hinder Our progress. I love you completely. Let us remove these final little blocks and be together so you can serve Me with abandon."

Of course the saints are the most powerful witnesses to how God's love can heal the human heart. Remember as you read, that some of these men and women were not saints all their lives. Some, like Augustine, had much experience of sinful love.

"O eternal truth, true love and beloved eternity. You are my God. To you do I sigh day and night. When I first came to know you, you drew me to yourself so that I might see that there were things for me to see, but that I myself was not yet ready to see them. Meanwhile you overcame the weakness of my vision, sending forth most strongly the beams of your light, and I trembled at once with love and dread... (Augustine found him in Christ and Holy Communion.)

"Late have I loved you, O Beauty ever ancient, ever new, late have I loved you! You were within me, but I was outside, and it was there that I searched for you. In my unloveliness I plunged into the lovely things which you created. You were with me, but I was not with you. Created things kept me from you; yet if they had not been in you they would not have been at all. I drew in breath and now I pant for you. I have tasted you, now I hunger and thirst for more. You touched me, and I burned for your peace."

Office of Readings pp. 1537-1538:
from *St. Augustine's Confessions*

From the writings of another saint,

"The law of love is not concerned with what will be, what ought to be, what can be. Love does not reflect; it is unreasonable and knows no moderation. Love refuses to be consoled when its goal proves impossible... Love destroys the lover if he cannot obtain what he loves; love follows its own promptings, and does not think of right and wrong... It is intolerable for love not to see the object of its longing. That is why whatever reward they merited was nothing to the saints if they could not see the Lord. A love that desires to see God may not have reasonableness on its side, but...it gave Moses the temerity to say: If I have found favor in your eyes, show me your face."

From St. Peter Chrysologus

And yet another,

"Many hear the world more easily than they heard God; they follow the desires of the flesh more readily than the pleasure of God. The world promises rewards that are temporal and insignificant, and these are pursued with great longing; I promise rewards that are eternal and unsurpassable, yet the hearts of mortals respond sluggishly. …my promise deceives no one, and leaves empty-handed no one who confides in me. What I have promised I shall give; what I have said I will fulfill for any man who remains faithful in my love unto the very end."

From The Office of Readings p. 1027:
from *The Imitation of Christ*

In a book about St. Therese of Lisieux, her biographer has many things to say that have reference to our themes:

"Thomas Aquinas would sum up the Christian life thus: 'Love did not permit God to remain alone.' So Therese thought of Jesus as a beggar for her love."

Fr. Bernard Bro, O.P., *St. Therese of Lisieux* (p. 92)

"Happiness is the possession, at once intense and peaceful, of all that we can desire." (p. 225)

"'God makes promises through his creatures and keeps them only through himself alone,' referring to how people promise to make us happy but they can't. He contrasts those who run after adventures leaping from one disappointment to the next and others who settle too low. We need the cross in order to want God alone..."

quote from Claudel (p. 227)

"Grace gives a thirst for God, for the beatitude of God and no other; the latter alone can henceforth satisfy our expectations, even if we do not know it. We can remain for a long time without knowing it, carry this seed for a long time in ourselves...an obscure uneasiness alerts us that in spite of a happy or passionate life we are not satisfied... One day this uneasiness becomes a call: ...something is waiting for us over there, very far away, and that this something is someone, and this someone is God... Then we realize that He is the happiness for which we are made." (p. 229)

"One day the love of God will force the gate of heaven...the love of God pursues us, in search of a heart that will open itself to him." (p. 233)

The great mystical Mexican holy woman, Venerable Conchita, wrote this:

"And if I experience this celestial life, why is it that I sometimes desire persons or things that are not He?... What is the benefit of filling myself with the smoke of human appreciation, vanity and self-love, which—alas!—diminish Jesus's presence in my soul? During the nights of my spirit, why do I look for affections that are taken by the wind, piercing the heart? Why build my nest in that which passes away and disappears, when here I have Him who always is? Oh, my god! I will no longer lose time on silly speculations and self-pleasure, in crazy illusions that stain the heart and hurt it vainly."

Conchita Cabrera de Armida, *Holy Hours*, 2005

I would like to end this long series of beautiful quotations by inviting you to make a complete surrender to God by means of a personal meditation I wrote some time ago:

The Center of Reality
A spinning ball of earth in a void of space? or
A huge heart with myriad rays of love—
one ray beaming into a heart with your name on it?

Meditate on this passage from Scripture:

"Who will separate us from the love of Christ? Trial, or distress, or persecution, or hunger, of nakedness, or danger, or the sword?... For I am certain that neither death nor life, neither angels nor principalities, neither the present nor the future, nor powers, neither height nor depth nor any other creature, will be able to separate us from the love of God that comes to us in Christ Jesus, our Lord."

Then go someplace where you can be alone with no interruptions from people or phones. Ask God to take you into the place in your heart of the deepest longing for love. Dwell in the pain for as long as you can. Then cry out, interiorly or out loud, "If you are a God of love, fill this place in my heart." Wait as long as you can. If you don't feel anything, repeat this meditation every day until you feel hope.

FORGIVENESS

"Healing begins when you abandon your demands for love and choose instead to give love, no matter what the cost. Madness, isn't it? But a madness that works…but first you have to forgive. Can you forgive your husband for failing to love you as you wish?"

From Michael O'Brien, *Strangers and Sojourners*

(p. 334)

Lynn and Pete

In any 12 Step Program there is a time when the participants work with their sponsors on reviewing their lives, forgiving those who have hurt them, and making amends to those they have hurt.

The one Lynn needed to forgive the most was her alcoholic husband. After going through this process she found that on the rare occasions she had to see him in connection with their sons she was able to greet him with a serene dignity instead of her previous nervous anticipation of a fight.

Lynn was dreading the process of having to forgive Pete. Even though she knew that he was not at fault and had done the right thing, there was still a sense of humiliation when memories would arise of that year of closeness followed by his dismissal of her. Lynn toyed with the idea of going to see him or writing him a long letter about how the whole thing felt from her point of view, maybe hinting he should be more careful in the future about being friendly with any other woman in the workplace.

Her sponsor suggested that it might rekindle feelings best left dormant to contact him again. Instead she suggested that Lynn write a never-to-be-sent letter including asking forgiveness for her own part in the disordered aspect of their friendship. Here is what Lynn wrote:

Dear Pete,

I still feel bad when I think of you. I wish that the day you broke off you had said something more like, "Lynn, you are a wonderful woman. I will miss meeting you for lunch. I am a loyal husband but I do love you as a friend." I want to forgive you for cutting me off kind of abruptly. I also want you to forgive me for pushing myself into your life more than a woman should do with a man who is married. It was a lonely time for me and I realize now I was sort of desperate. I hope that your whole life is very happy and that as I heal from my unhappy marriage, my life will be happier also.

After re-reading the letter a few times she brought it to the Eucharistic Adoration chapel in her parish Church and offered it to Jesus and then tore it up and threw it in the waste paper basket.

Accomplishing these steps with respect to Pete gave her a feeling of greater lightness and also forgiveness of herself for her part in that embarrassing period.

Matt and Joey

Years after the events chronicled in our story, there was a parish mission during Lent at Matt's Church. Matt and Carol sat next to each other in the pew. The priest began to talk about the importance of forgiveness. "Who is the person in all your lifetime you need to forgive most?" Matt looked around at his wife and picked up that her candidate would probably be himself! It took him awhile to think of Joey as the one who hurt himself most because they had been getting along pretty well, especially because Matty, the first grandson, seemed to like baseball.

"Now, folks, no matter how hard it is, I want you to make a list in your mind of the worst ways this person hurt you."

Matt thought, *That Joey didn't even discuss it with me when he went for that art scholarship for college?... That he never thanked me for all those years of coaching and coming to his games?*

"Now, I want you to ask God to give you a hint why He allowed this person to do this to you."

That's a hard one, Matt thought. *I've never believed God has to let you in on His reasons... Hmmm... So I could let go of Joey and give attention to all those other kids in the high school who desperately need fatherly help?... So I would realize I needed a closer walk with you, Jesus? Maybe I was a little too proud before?*

"Now," boomed the voice of the priest, "picture the person who hurt you most and then say to him or her in your heart—I forgive you."

Matt did say those words, but his musings on this spiritual exercise were interrupted as his wife, Carol, with tears in her eyes, grabbed him by the arms to turn his body toward hers. Then came a big hug and the words, "I forgive you for everything, Matt. Yes, I really do."

Tom and Cathy

Only insiders know how important the ordination to the diaconate is for seminarians. It is at that ordination, prior to the one to the priesthood, that they make their vows never to marry. It was at the one-week long retreat prior to his ordination as deacon that Tom put the final period to his fantasies about Cathy. Even though she married Alex a year before this ordination, until the actual vow, Tom could still daydream about what might change if Alex were to die suddenly.

The Franciscan priest who was leading the retreat insisted that each seminarian present had let God purify his soul by making an act of forgiveness of past hurts. "I wouldn't want to be the parishioner who is unlucky enough to look like dear old Dad, and become the beneficiary of your non-forgiving anger."

As a preparation for this healing, it was suggested that each of the deacon candidates write at the top of a piece of paper the one quality he disliked the most in other people. Tom had no trouble: coldness!

Then they were told to make a list of everyone they had ever known who exemplified that quality. On Tom's list was first his father, then a high school teacher, and then Fr. John, his first spiritual director in the Franciscans and a few other fathers in the Order.

"Now pray to the Holy Spirit to give you wisdom about

what causes this negative trait in people. I'll give you a good half hour to figure this one out."

On Tom's sheet of paper were notes like these: "The cold person was himself treated coldly as a child?—Grandpa was just as cold as Dad." "Men think they have to be cold or they become as mushy as women?" "Hot is too scary?"

Now the retreat director draped his long, lean body further over the lectern. "Okay, guys, here's the point. Can you forgive those who hurt you for that trait now that you have a better idea where it comes from?... Just say 'I forgive you' in your heart right now even if you don't want to. If you want to forgive, that's enough for God to work with."

Lastly, the seminarians had to write thank you notes, to be sent or not at their discretion, to all those people who had helped them heal from the wounds of the past. Here are some lines from those Tom wrote with tears in his eyes:

"Dear Dr. Greg, thank you for that time you spent as my counselor. I would never have been able to become a deacon or a priest without your compassion and insight."

"Dear Cathy, maybe I loved you too much for a seminarian, but I sure am glad you were there to be my friend. After I become a priest, I am counting on you and Alex to give me a surrogate family to visit where I can just be myself."

A highlight of Tom's ordination to the priesthood was when he laid his hands in blessing on the head of his father.

When Tom saw the tears of joy in his father's eyes, he believed that the flame of his act of forgiveness had somehow melted the hard heart of that feared man.

—Analysis of Forgiveness—

Now it's your turn, dear reader. Go through the same forgiveness exercises our characters went through, putting in the names of those you felt rejected by. Here are the challenges they were given:

Make a list of all those who have hurt you, and then go through the list one by one and try to forgive them.

Make a list of all those you have hurt. Ask forgiveness directly if possible, or symbolically if not in a never-to-be-sent letter, of those you have hurt.

Who is the person you need to forgive the most? What good does it seem God might have had in mind in allowing you to go through the pain that person caused you? What is the quality you dislike the most in other people? What might be some of the causes of that trait? Can you forgive those who hurt you with that trait? Thank those who have helped you heal your wounds.

Does all this talk of forgiveness seem too facile to you, perhaps? Are you being told that forgiveness is easy and quickly over with? It is understandable if you have these doubts. I have written these pages about forgiveness to give you an impetus to begin the process. Willing to forgive is half the battle. What is the alternative? Nourishing feelings of failure, misery, anger, resentment, desire for revenge?

No one is to be blamed for feeling deeply wounded by the rejection of others. In the world as God wished it to be there would have been no human rejection. We would have felt total love every moment of our lives and we would not have any defects that could provoke rejection either.

The life and example of Jesus, our Redeemer, shows us that even if a person had absolutely nothing worthy of rejection about him, there could still be rejection! And yet He had the most to forgive.

If this chapter just seems too much to take in now, go on to the next and come back to the forgiveness exercises when you feel more open to them.

LOVE

"Nothing is certain, but everything is safe.
That is part of the mystery of love."
Charles Williams, *The Greater Trumps* (p. 191)

Lynn

Let us look at the life of our fictional character Lynn five years after the events narrated in the previous chapters. This woman, now forty-seven years old, spends most of her time at her job with Catholic Charities doing counseling of the needy who apply for advice and aid. She earned an M.A. in family counseling at night while acquainting herself with the ministry of Catholic Charities as an assistant to an administrator. Partly because of her problems with her alcoholic husband, Lynn finds a wealth of sympathy for her clients and much satisfaction in being able to help them on the road to healing and better coping mechanisms. Because it is a Catholic organization, she can pray with people in need and also with the staff.

Lynn continues to attend co-dependency meetings to check her own tendencies to unrealistic expectations in relationships with men. Her 12 Step group helped her see that dating another heavy drinker who seemed on the verge of recovery but never quite made it was a big mistake. Presently she is seriously dating another counselor, a widower, also with grown adult children. They go together to a noon Mass at the Catholic Charities chapel offering themselves to Jesus and asking Him to give them the wisdom to accept each other's limitations and not to pressure each other to perfectly fulfill their fantasies.

When, from time to time, Lynn thinks of Pete, it is with rueful humor. She has stopped blaming him or herself for the rejection.

Matt

On their twenty-fifth wedding anniversary Matt and Carol were reminiscing about the good and bad in their past years together. Carol was able to joke about her fear that Matt might have sunk into such depression over Joey's rebellion that she would be stuck with a sexless marriage. For his part, Matt was able to affirm Carol for seeing him through that rough period of his life. Though at first he found it contrary to his macho image to have a wife working outside the home, now he enjoys the extra money. They use it for weekend vacations and trips to see Dee and Joey and the grandchildren.

Matt likes to witness to other Knights of Columbus going through mid-life depression about how good it was for him to change jobs. He had no idea until coaching at the high school how many of the kids, girls as well as boys, were without fathers in the home and how eager they were for his support and advice.

Even though he doesn't really understand art, Matt politely affirms Joe when his son shows him the graphics he does for a large company's website and training programs. In turn, when Matt and Carol visit, Joe listens for hours to Matt recounting the successful games of his high school teams.

Father Tom

When Fr. John, Tom's first spiritual director, reminisces with the other older friars, he likes to boast of having always thought Tom was going to be a winner. "When I'd done all I could, Dr. Greg took over and brought him through that vocation crisis."

Father Tom, still overweight, still a little insecure, got outstanding evaluations from the young people in the large youth ministry group he leads in the Franciscan parish. The teens appreciate his warmth and sensitivity.

Five years after his ordination, Tom does quite a bit of spiritual direction with new seminarians. Talking this role over with Dr. Greg, he has come to see how God worked through his childhood wounds to make him the good priest and counselor he is now. Closeness to his nurturing mother gave him a model for being loving to those he ministers to now. The estrangement from his father gave him a desperation for fatherly love that drove him into the arms of God the Father. In celebrating Mass, the element of the priest representing Christ the Son in worship of the Father is especially real to Tom.

Not that there is never a psychological crisis. When Tom is forced to be in daily contact with any male authority figure who is cold or sarcastic, the old feelings of fear of rejection come back. It helps Tom to make an emergency appointment with Dr. Greg to work it through. The process involves realizing that the old father wound has been opened again, accepting the pain, and giving it to Jesus. Then he is counseled to overcome his fear and be assertive enough to confront the offensive male in a polite but firm manner.

For instance, the pastoral associate supervising youth ministry liked to ridicule one of Tom's pet programs. Dr. Greg coaxed Tom into making an appointment with that authority figure. "Mr. Koharski," Tom was able to say, "I realize that my methods are different from the ones you would choose were you running youth ministry, so you are naturally skeptical, but I've tried this a few times with success. I would be more comfortable if you wouldn't joke about my method in front of the kids." It worked.

Just as Tom had hoped, once he became committed to the priestly vocation, Tom was able to accept Cathy's husband, Alex, and get to know and like him better. Cathy is still his best friend and their little children love visits from Father Tom.

—Analysis of Love—

Healing of rejection comes through love—real love. This real love comes from God directly and also from those He puts in our lives to be channels of that love. Since we are imperfect channels at best, the love we get from others is never perfectly fulfilling, but can still be nourishing and healing. St. Thomas Aquinas taught that we can only love ourselves loving. This means that we need to have persons in our lives to love, despite all our failings, if we are to enjoy being the persons we are called by God to be.

Because of feelings of rejection stemming all the way from early childhood, many of us enter into relationships with unreal fantasies of compensation for previous wounds, or anxiety about fresh rejections. We may put up walls around ourselves to get as much love as we can with the least amount of pain.

If we surrender to the perfect healing love of God, we will find the Holy Spirit giving us hints about how to renew old bonds on a healthier basis, and how to create new bonds that are less disappointing. Especially we may need to heed warnings about gravitating to just the sorts of people who are most likely to reject us again. Those of us who, in spite of a strong Christian life in the sacraments and prayer, find ourselves repeating such destructive patterns will usually need psychological and/or spiritual counsel from experts if we are to change for the better.

I once consulted an expert in healing about my tendency to latch onto rejecting male figures. Even though I had some good relationships with other men, including having a husband with much love in his heart for me in spite of conflicts, I would start up intense friendships with colder men. The mentor suggested that because my father seemed cold and rejecting of me as a child, I might think I didn't deserve a loving male in my life. So I could punish myself for having some of this highly desired love by balancing it with a rejecting male friend. Pretty complicated! Certainly more than I could cope with. The counsel of therapists at various times of crisis, as well as a longer period of psychoanalysis in my early sixties, brought much insight and some healing. Now I am better able to detect the recurring pattern and disengage myself more quickly, often retaining the good parts of those friendships or at least not carrying bitterness for years afterwards.

In our narratives about our main fictional characters I have included elements of the healing power of real love. What are some of those signs of real love as opposed to distorted bondings? Let's look at realistic vs. fanciful expectations; good communication vs. habitual repression of negative feelings and theories; helping vs. withholding; willingness to forgive; and humor.

What is described under these subtitles, by the way, is sometimes relevant only to adult bonds. Parent/child interactions involve duties of formation with their own special obligations.

Realistic vs. Fanciful Expectations

In a self-help group on mental health called Recovery, Inc. (not 12 Step) founded by Abraham Low, there is an emphasis on expecting the average from others vs. the desired exceptional. If my friend is usually late, I should expect this whenever we have an appointment vs. fantasizing that he or she will come early or on time and then feeling frustrated and angry. Most children are messy. I should expect my children to be messy. I may need to discipline them to be more tidy, but I shouldn't think that just because I love neatness, they will love it, too. If my spouse is a more introverted person who needs quiet and space, I should not bombard him or her with cheerful chatter the minute he or she walks in the door. If my spouse is an anxious person, I should not demand courageous confrontation in situations where it might be good but is not absolutely necessary.

All psychologists agree that trying to build relationships on the idea that I will be able to change the other person's character is a recipe for anger and disappointment. People can change over time—usually a long, long time—but because they really want to, not because I want them to.

What is the Christian perspective on this? It is prideful to demand perfection in others, as if we could control them. It is humble to patiently deal with the limitations of others, hoping they will also be patient with ours.

Sometimes someone looks better than he or she is at the onset of a relationship. In the case of the emergence of extreme evil, addictive, or psychotic behavior, we have a right to flee. That is realistic. It is unrealistic to think that we can fix those with such problems. Sometimes, with the grace of God, they will be miraculously transformed. We can pray for this. But we can't expect it as if just because it would be better for us, it has to happen.

Good Communication vs. Repression of Conflict

Some of us are afraid of honest expression of our thoughts and feelings. Since some of these are negative, we imagine that trying to push them aside and get on with life will be less dangerous or hurtful. Whereas psychologists warn against violently physical or verbal explosions, they all agree that repressing our feelings damages love. How so? Bottling up bad emotions does not destroy them; they just fester below the surface. The result can be distancing, or coldness, which are forms of REJECTION.

Even though some friendships and even family bonds may have to be broken because of unresolvable conflicts, many will improve if there is honest but loving communication. This is especially true if there is ample affirmation as a staple. "Dear one, here are all the things I love about you (list them)," followed by, "but there is this one thing I am having difficulty with now," is very different from, "You are a (blankety-blank) bad person. I hate you. Change, or else."

"Perfect love casts out fear." (1 John 4:18) Sheltered in the protective love of God, we need to prudently and lovingly open ourselves to each other in our often muddled reaction to daily problems.

Helpfulness vs. Withholding

Given the difficulties of life, real love will always involve serving others in a multitude of ways: physical, emotional, and spiritual. A sure sign of lack of real love is someone who professes to love us deeply but never helps when we are in need.

How healing it is when we feel rejected if someone, even a

stranger, helps us in even the smallest need, such as picking up a dropped object, or a smile from the cashier at the check-out counter.

Real love has to involve some manifestation in helpfulness, but a problem that has recently been analyzed is that there are different ways to show such love. My way may not be your way. When you don't show love the way I would, I may unnecessarily feel neglected. In the book *The Five Languages of Love*, Gary Chapman describes these manifestations:

- Words of affirmation
- Quality time
- Giving gifts
- Acts of service
- Touch

All of these fall under trying to help the beloved person, but they are not the same. If you want to check yourself, why not jot down on a piece of paper all through a week how many times you affirm someone; give them quality time; give a gift, offer physical help, or touch them in a tender manner (of course, one acceptable to the recipient).

In real love, we become sensitive to the ways the other shows love to us and also become willing to show it to them, not only in our favorite way, but in another mode if that one is especially needed. For example, even if you were not brought up to be affectionate it would be withholding to refrain from holding a family member or friend who was in tears. If I love to give gifts but another needs an emergency ride to the hospital more than a present, it would be withholding to refuse. A busy person's expression of love through opening up a good long time to listen to someone who needs advice can be a great sign of love.

Jesus tells us that we must show our love by laying down our lives for each other. Real love takes this seriously and is willing to stretch beyond personal preference wherever the need is greatest.

Forgiveness

Forgiveness of rejection was the subject of the last chapter. Here I only want to insist that even where rejection is not in question, there can be no love between sinful human beings that is not based on forgiveness, 70x7 if necessary. Real love does not demand perfection from the other.

Humor

Real love is not a ponderous affair of perpetual controlling and resentment. If you watch strangers, say in a restaurant, it is easy to see where the love is because of the laughter.

In this regard the signs of real love already mentioned come together. People with unrealistic expectations are usually mad, not enjoyable. Those who repress communication become sullen, not funny. Withholding of help leads to feelings of deprivation in the other, not of grateful joy. Those who forgive each other for limitations laugh at the same things they previously berated each other for.

From a Christian standpoint, if I know Jesus as my real Savior, I don't have to be so dependent on others to make my life happy. I go to them not with desperate thirst, but with tenderness and thankfulness for whatever they can do to lighten the burdens of my life. If we don't have to save one another, we can laugh a lot more.

Here are some quotations about real love you might find provocative and inspiring. They are not arranged chronologically by date of authorship but vary contemporary with perennial expressions of truth about real love.

"Dear children, you were each created by the Father. He takes the greatest joy in watching your progress as you learn how to love during your time in the world. You experience difficulties in this regard but you overcome these difficulties and you grow and advance. This process of learning to love and rejecting all that is not love is the real point of your time on earth.

"If you were told that you would be coming to

heaven soon, how would you treat the souls around you? How would you view them differently if you knew that your time with them was limited? Well, little souls, I am reminding you today that your time with each of the souls around you is finite. Time will pass and your time with that soul will be over. If you love each soul in your life, you will be at peace when your time together is finished. You will feel satisfaction in that you will know that you tried to love them, despite the difficulties that arose to make this challenging.

"These difficulties or obstacles to love originate from two sources. One source of difficulty is your own failings and the other source of difficulty is the failings of the other soul. These difficulties, which are expected, must be overcome so that you can treat each other with the pure love that you will experience in heaven...

"If you had to do this alone, you would surely struggle and possibly find yourself without the forgiveness necessary to love each other as we love in heaven. But you do not proceed alone. You proceed with all of heaven and with Me, Jesus Christ.

"I have given you many examples of how I loved during My time on earth. Read about Me in

Scripture, dear apostles, and then be gentle as I was gentle. Be kind as I was kind. Be respectful as I was respectful. Be forgiving as I was forgiving.

"I am with you in each moment and you may ask me for the grace to love each soul in your life. In this process, you will find great joy. This joy is only the very beginning of My reward to you. Be at peace. Your God created you to love and He will teach you how to do this."

From the writings of Anne, a Lay Apostle who believes that these words were given to her by Jesus, December, 2005

"(I need to) be gentle with my own needs and wants. Avoid obsessing over others' faults, which prevent me from focusing on my unhealthy behavior. Need for play, feel grief about disappointments… Not just change the place or people, since it is in me the problems are. Avoid expecting a perfect someone. I need to meet my own needs plus help from trustworthy people. Have my own self-definition vs. parent tapes of who I am."

CoDa Newcomers Guide (p. 53)

More from CoDa wisdom:

Unless you find that you are able to bring others, with the help of God or counseling (for instance marriage counseling), to improve these behaviors, you need to avoid as much as possible those who exhibit traits such as these:

- Neglect—doesn't return calls, not available, lets you down;
- Coldness—facial expressions of disdain, no appropriate affection when you are fragile;
- Exploitation—since you won't leave the other can ask you to do anything anytime;
- Sarcasm—disdain, demeaning, sometimes harsh teasing; or sometimes physical abuse.

"A twofold wish carries all love towards its accomplishment. On the one hand, the wish not to be alone anymore and, for that purpose, the wish that the other might be, first of all, truly, a partner."

Fr. Bernard Bro, O.P.,
St. Therese of Lisieux (p. 75)

"We can't load all of our need for emotional sustenance and spiritual meaning into a single relationship. God didn't make us that way. Whether we focus all our need for affection and support on a spouse or even on God himself, we are bound to be disappointed—and the temptation may be irresistible to turn elsewhere, to unsanctioned human relationships, to fill the void. This is not because God cannot meet our emotional needs. Rather, he has designed us to have them met in a range of human relationships."

From Chris Armstrong:

www.christianitytoday.com/ct/2004137/52.0.html

"When your heart is torn with grief, the Lord hears you."

Liturgy of the Hours, Saturday Week 3

Daytime prayer

"He taught us to love him by first loving us, even to death on the cross. By loving us and holding us so dear, He stirred us to love Him who had first loved us to the end. ...not because You needed our love, but because we could not be what You create us to be, except by loving You.

"...You know that this disposition (love) could not be forced on men's hearts, my God, since You created them; it must rather be elicited. And this, for the further reason that there is no freedom where there is compulsion, and where freedom is lacking, so too is righteousness... From the beginning of creation it was He (the Holy Spirit) who hovered over the waters—that is, over the wavering minds of men, offering Himself to all, drawing all things to Himself."

From William of Saint Thierry, Abbot,

Office of Readings (p. 46)

"I desire to have such a perfect attainment of chaste love that I would be a comfort to somebody harassed by their own inner agony, a safe haven to someone sore beset. I would like to look at another person with deep tenderness, and not with desperate neediness. I'd like to be the kind of woman who can liberate with a laugh, who can inspire love for holiness —for You, Lord—with a look or a very few words."

Julianne Loesch Wiley, *Emma* (p. 118)

Conclusion

"Ponder on your bed and be still
'What can bring happiness?' many say.
Let the light of your face shine on us,
O Lord You have put into my heart a greater joy
Than they have from abundance of corn and new wine.
I will lie down in peace and sleep comes at once
For you alone, Lord, make me dwell in safety."

(Psalm 4)

As I finish writing my little and heartfelt book about surviving rejection with the help of God, I am thinking of two possible readers. One of them is thanking God and me because the stories and insights in the book have helped give him or her hope in a troubled and intensely painful part of life.

Another is thinking, "Yes...but:

- "My rejections have been much worse than those described" or
- "Even though the remedies sound good, I don't believe I will ever be free of this recurring torment" or
- "I just never seem to be attracted to those wholesome, good, loving people who will not reject me."

To those of you with such objections, my best wisdom is to throw yourself into the arms of Jesus with the same gusty intensity you throw yourself into promising relationships. Ask Him to give you the trust to believe that immediately or slowly but surely He can bring you healing.

When I began to work on *Healing of Rejection,* I was wondering who could be a good patron saint for this particular form of suffering. Let me tell you about Blessed Margaret of Castello. I dare you to think you have suffered worse!

It was in the 14th century in Italy that a military man and his wife gave birth to a little girl born blind, lame, dwarfed, and hunchbacked. The parents were so distressed that they decided to pretend she had died in childbirth and hide her away in a remote room of their castle.

Noticing that the girl, as she grew up, loved to pray, and

worrying that it would be impossible to hide her forever, these parents thought of a way to make sure the secret didn't get out. As was sometimes done with pious adult women, they put her in a room adjoining the chapel where she could be locked in but still see the Mass and receive Holy Communion. This cell was freezing in the winter and suffocating in the summer. Just the same, with the help of a loving chaplain, little deformed Margaret became a loving contemplative.

Hearing of a miraculous cure in a Church in the town of Castello, the parents made up their minds to bring the now twenty-year-old Margaret to the shrine, but when no miracle occurred they abandoned her on the steps of the Church with the beggars.

First the beggars befriended Margaret and then others who became impressed by the way this unfortunate woman brought peace and love to whoever she encountered. Eventually, she became a Third Order Dominican Mantellate—consecrated but not a formal nun. She visited the sick with many miraculous cures, attended the dying and became an instrument of Jesus in the conversion of prisoners. She would be seen levitating into the air, hands folded in prayer. Though still blind, she memorized the psalms and could see Christ in the Eucharist during the Mass.

St. Margaret's story illustrates that the miseries of rejection need not be the end of the story for us. With God's help we

can become wounded healers, as Henri Nouwen's famous book
by that title suggests.

BIBLIOGRAPHY

"About Co-Dependents Anonymous"—from their Newcomer's Handbook (Dallas: CoDA Publishing Enterprise, 1994)

Andric, Ivo, *The Bridge on the Drina* (Chicago: University of Chicago Press, 1977.)

Bossis, Gabrielle, *He and I* (Boston: Pauline Books, 1988)

Bro, Fr. Bernard, O.P., *St. Therese of Lisieux* (San Francisco: Ignatius Press, 2003)

Butler, David, *Disraeli: Portrait of a Romantic*, (New York: Warner Books, 1978)

Cantalamessa, Raniero Article published in Rome, JUNE 17, 2005 (Zenit.org)—ZE05061703

Chapman, Gary, *The Five Languages of Love* (Moody Press, 1992)

Howatch, Susan, *The Heartbreaker* (New York: Knopf, 2004)

Hughes, Ted, *Collected Poems* edited by Paul Keegan (NY Farrar, Straus and Giroux, 2003)

Ludwig, Emil, *Napoleon* (New York: Modern Library, 1915)

Martel, Yann, *Life of Pi* (Edinburgh: Canongate Books, 2002)

O'Brien, Michael, *Father Elijah* (San Francisco: Ignatius Press, 1996) *Strangers and Sojourners* (San Francisco: Ignatius Press, 2002)

Office of Readings (Boston: St. Paul Editions, 1993)

Rivera-Garza, *No One Will See Me Cry* (trans. Andrew Hurley Willimantic, Ct.: Curbstone Press, 2003)

Viorst, Judith, *Necessary Losses: The Loves, Illusions, Dependencies and Impossible Expectations That All of Us Have to Give Up in Order to Grow* (New York: Fawcett, 1986)

Wiley, Julianne Loesch, *Emma,* manuscript, 2004

Williams, Charles, *The Greater Trumps* (Grand Rapids, Michigan: Wm. B. Eerdman's Publishing Company, 1976)

Witness Stories

To make *Healing of Rejection* a little more complete, I asked people with striking stories of rejection to write me short accounts. Many of them found it too painful to write about rejection. Others wanted to write about how God helped them survive and heal, but only under names other than their own. Here they are.

From Caroline Price

After more than twenty-eight years of marriage and five children, I found myself one day in the living room with my husband. He was in a state familiar to me: confrontational, belligerent and arrogant. I braced myself for the verbal onslaught that was sure to come. Without preamble he said, "You are no longer a part of my life. Don't try to change my mind."

I thought, *You have lost your mind!*

He said, "Don't try to lay guilt on me. I like the life I've chosen."

I asked myself, *What life? Where has he been living besides here?*

He continued, "I feel stifled. I need space."

How trite. Indignantly I countered with, "I have given you the whole world except for the spot I occupy, and look what you have done with it!"

Not believing that our life together could be over in an instant I asked, "Can't we work this out? I'll go with you to marriage counseling, psychological counseling, or any remedial program you choose."

He replied, "No. My decision is final. I never have been faithful to you. Men are not suited to monogamy."

Stunned, I had no reply. He was speaking in terms beyond my comprehension.

As I have said, we had been married for more than twenty-eight years when this transpired. We had five children, all living independently. Over time, we had progressed from penury to prosperity, and he was a professional with an excellent reputation in our community. For this reason, he wanted me to continue to live in the same house, act as his hostess, maintain social and business relationships, prepare for and join in family festivities and behave as though nothing had changed between us. I was to keep up appearances in return for my status as his wife and a comfortable life in a prestigious neighborhood, but with no conjugal rights.

At this proposal, something in me snapped. I said, "Oh no— you can't fire me; I quit! I can understand how that lifestyle would be ideal for you, but for me it would be intolerable. I'm gone!"

This is a classic example of an "Aha experience!" After more than twenty-eight years of marriage it took less than twenty-eight seconds for me to make that decision.

As I gazed upon this man who had been an almost constant companion for more than half of my life, he underwent a metamorphosis into a stranger. Truly, I felt as though all through those years I had been married to a total stranger. In a flash, my mind's eye envisioned what I took to be his soul, corrupted by a careless life of debauchery. Like the portrait of Dorian Gray, it was not a pretty sight, and I was repelled. The man with whom I had shared my love, my hopes, my fears, my aspirations—all that I was or ever hoped to be had proved to be a figment of my imagination.

And so we went our separate ways. After eighteen months of living apart, we were granted a divorce on grounds of irreconcilable differences and I was left to grapple with the wreckage of my most unnatural disaster: rejection.

Few occurrences in life are as emphatic and dramatic as the end of a marriage in divorce when one partner has been rejected. So I found myself dwelling in the catacombs of buried memories, peering into niches containing crumbling remnants that once had glowed with the vitality of a cherished past. Harbingers of loving times to come were no more. Echoes of anguish faded, because I no longer had the psychic energy to produce a whimper, much less a wail. My heart hardened; there were no tears left to keep it supple. This is the human condition of a heart and soul deprived of the nourishment of love; the habitat of the rejected.

The human spirit cannot sustain a mood indefinitely; there comes a time when it must move on, or expire. Some can prolong the agony, choosing to live in a twilight zone engulfed in self-pity and self-loathing to the end. Others, more hopeful, will manage to escape from their quagmires of despondency and struggle to understand what had gone wrong. They will act upon the principle of examining the past so as not to repeat its errors.

Fortunately for me, I fell into the latter category and became engrossed in dredging up past events that should have served as a foreshadowing of the dissolution of my marriage. I began by analyzing characteristics I had assumed were basic to sustaining a relationship that would flourish: mutual affection, trustworthiness, honesty, responsibility. In the beginning, our marriage was based upon all of these, or so I thought.

But when did the quality of our life together begin to disintegrate? Applying the perfect vision of hindsight, I could see the answer clearly: when my husband began to consort with persons unknown to me. On occasion, my presence was required at social events in which they were included. I began to realize that their values were corrupt: they over-indulged in alcohol, experimented with drugs, swapped and/or cheated on their spouses, viewed lewd movies, engaged in vile conversations, and were generally depraved in their private lives. When I refused to condone their behavior, my husband seemingly agreed to terminate all contact with them.

However, he chose to continue living the lifestyle undercover. Using various subterfuges, he lived a double life. His demand for us to live in such a way that he could have the best of both worlds came when he no longer had the will or the way to maintain the double life in which he had become enmeshed. Purely and simply, he could not serve two masters.

This may sound melodramatic to readers with no experience of living in the sixties. It was a period when for the first time middle America was exposed to the phenomena of X-rated movies, open marriage, readily available "social drugs," oral contraceptives, pornography, Playboy Clubs (even in rural areas), and I'm sure many occasions of immorality that I never had heard of (and, please God, never will). So a charge of hyperbole is not applicable here.

I still don't know if my lack of awareness stemmed from denial, self-deception or repression; perhaps all of the above. However, a reading from the *Book of Wisdom* made clear to me why there could be no reconciliation unless my husband made a firm resolution to reform his lifestyle:

"The wicked said among themselves,
thinking not aright:

"'Let us beset the just one, because he is obnoxious
to us; he sets himself against our doings,
Reproaches us for transgressions of the law and
charges us with violations of our training.
He professes to have knowledge of God
and styles himself a child of the Lord.
To us he is the censure of our thoughts;
merely to see him is a hardship for us,
Because his life is not like other men's,
and different are his ways.
He judges us debased;
he holds aloof from our paths as from things impure.
He calls blest the destiny of the just
and boasts that God is his Father.
Let us see whether his words be true;
let us find out what will happen to him.

For if the just one be the son of God,

he will defend him

And deliver him from the hand of his foes.

With revilement and torture let us put him to the test

that we may have proof of his gentleness

and try his patience.

Let us condemn him to a shameful death;

for according to his own words,

God will take care of him.'

"These were their thoughts, but they erred;

for their wickedness blinded them,

And they knew not the hidden counsels of God;

neither did they count on a recompense of holiness

nor discern the innocent soul's reward."

Wisdom 2:12-22

I believe that on some level my husband understood this, which caused him to say, "Don't try to lay guilt on me." His very last words to me were, "You will probably come out of this better than I will."

It takes time to come to the realization that the perfect, unconditional love of Christ is there for the taking to soothe the heart, and that the gift of "our daily bread" in the Eucharist is available to nourish the soul. We were not created to dwell in a hell of our own making. But we must take the initiative to seek remedies of the healing of our souls. We must strive to know God, for to know Him is to love Him. We must relinquish our postures of self-pity and resume our positions as servants/handmaids of the Lord. Only by doing this can we restore our self-respect and dignity, thus regaining inner peace and abundant love for others.

But being weak and unskilled in the methods of restoring my soul, I continued stumbling blindly along the road back to "normalcy" in darkness, heedless of the pitfalls. What a fool I was! I had only to ask the Light of the World for illumination; I had only to reach out and touch Christ's robe to be cured. But my impoverished spiritual condition rendered me incapable of following that line of reasoning. As the saying goes: welcome to the human race.

I was living in a state of mental and emotional desolation when the death blow to my marriage was delivered silently, by mail: A FINAL DECREE IN THE MATTER OF etc., etc., etc. No wounds, no bruises, no visible proof of violence was apparent. Death resulted from internal injuries felt only by the rejected and known only to God.

I searched my soul asking, "What enigma is this?" How can one live year after year blindly believing, hoping, praying for the grace of endurance to no avail? I only longed for us to live out our lives together in this "valley of tears," this "exile," so that at last our souls could be delivered into the arms of Mary and her Beloved Son. This was a goal I sincerely believed was attainable. However, I had failed to take into account that for any goal to be reached in tandem, both participants must strive for the same objective. As in all else, I must forge on alone. But no, not alone; rather as a needy member of the communion of saints.

Eventually I was able to absorb the impact of the breakup of my marriage. However, it took quite some time for me to restore my equanimity and to overcome the tendency to slip into a state of self-pity and denial that characteristically accompanies depression.

Gradually, I came to terms with the reality of my altered state of being. But I had to deal with the ramifications of no longer being one of a couple, but merely one. This presented a distinctly different set of causes of inner turmoil which were even less tolerable than those related to rejection by my spouse.

I found myself the object of pity, scorn and/or benign neglect, depending on the attitude toward divorce of the person involved. Some well-meaning friends offered uninformed advice; others tried to give me moral support by glorifying me and vilifying "him" ("he" no longer being dignified by his name). I was also subjected to contrived "encounters" with eligible bachelors who were not in and of themselves objectionable, but completely bizarre as companions for me (not to mention that I, as a divorced Catholic, was in no way eligible to marry anyone).

I wish that I could say that I dealt with these trials and tribulations by seeking refuge in the Lord and contemplating the numerous rejections suffered by Christ. Much to my detriment, such was not the case. Many years passed, during which I needlessly suffered countless heartaches. This is proof positive to me that intelligence does not preclude stupidity.

With the need to support myself, I became increasingly drawn into a self-absorbed frame of mind. I became preoccupied with striving for professional recognition and a secure place in the milieu of the divorced. In the process, I became increasingly alienated from the Church and all that is holy.

The turning point came for me one evening in a sumptuous apartment on the twentieth floor of a high-rise overlooking New York City. When I accepted an invitation to a dinner party there, my host gave me a time a half hour prior to his other guests. Although we had been to various entertainments in the city, I had never been in his condo, so he showed me around. He was doing the cooking and left me in front of a picture window with a stunning view of the city while he checked the food. The thought came to me: It must have been like this for Christ when the devil tempted Him in the desert.

My friend had come back to stand behind me. He said, "We could have a wonderful life together here."

Without hesitation, I replied, "What does it profit a man if he gains the whole world and suffers the loss of his own soul?"

With that, I heard him gasp, and I turned toward him. His face was ashen, and he said, "You are too chaste for me." I discovered later that he had spent three years in a Catholic seminary. We are still friends; I pray for him, and I hope he prays for me.

When I left that place, I not only returned to my earthly home, but I also resumed my journey to my heavenly home. The pain of rejection is a thing of the past. I am sometimes asked if I would remarry. My answer is this: If you can show me a man whose love for me can equal that of the love that Christ has for me, I might consider him. So far no one has materialized.

From "Magdalene"

I have been asked to share my story with you. But it is not my story, it is His. As St. Paul says, "By God's grace, I am what I am." It is all His work, not mine.

I am one of five children, born into a family with no Christian values. My father was baptized Catholic, but hadn't practiced his faith since he left home at a young age. My mother was raised in a Protestant family, but she didn't practice her faith as an adult either. The only time God was ever called upon in our home was amidst cussing and yelling.

My siblings and I suffered much abuse at the hands of our parents growing up. Our alcoholic father was always laid off, so money being tight put a strain on their marriage. This, along with both parents being brought up in abusive homes themselves, led to their physical and emotional abuse of us. I always said I understood and forgave them, not realizing the degree of suppressed anger and scars that lay deep within.

My lifetime memories are full of big holes, especially the first ten years or so, which are totally blank. The only memories I recall of my teen years are those of being beaten, or that of my own sinfulness, but nothing positive. The coping mechanism I had developed as a child affected my memory and I continued to block things without realizing it. Even the memories I have now as an adult are few.

I never really knew what love was, but can anyone unless they have first received it? I don't remember ever being told I was loved by my parents, nor were there any signs of affection in our home. The only touches I ever received were from the back of a hand or a belt.

Our house was a house from hell where yelling, cussing, hitting, and using God's name in vain was the norm. The put downs were as constant as the beatings. A common phrase was, "You no-good-for-nothing-son-of-a-b..." I believed I was no good. I never had any friends or invited anyone to our house, for I was afraid of them seeing the truth of what lied within.

When a child does not find love and security at home, he or she usually goes looking for it elsewhere. I found myself hanging out with my older sister and her friends, experimenting with drugs. I didn't enjoy what I was experiencing, BUT it got me out of THAT house, for I feared my father's drunken wrath! Then boys began to enter the picture... But I was taken advantage of and "date raped." There was a male friend I had throughout high school; after we graduated he raped me, too. I developed a friendship with a girl in my senior year, but she later betrayed me. There was even a member of my extended family who tried to molest me.

I developed a mistrust for everyone and became deeply introverted. I built walls around myself to protect me and didn't let anyone, or anything, in or out. These walls became a real handicap, for I was so withdrawn I couldn't speak. The words would go round and round in my head but it was as though there was a short circuit and I couldn't get them to my lips.

For some reason I had always been attracted to the Catholic kids at school. So after marrying a cradle Catholic, I converted. But it wasn't until we had children and began to teach them their religion that I began to understand what it was I professed at Mass on Sunday.

Our marriage was surviving, but that was about it. We weren't the best of friends as we should have been. I was busy raising our children while he was either working or spending time with his best friend. Whenever he had something bothering him, it was to this friend he confided, not me. I was deeply hurt knowing I'd never be first in his life, but realized there was nothing I could do but accept it. Needless to say, there I remained, that unloved little girl, rejected over and over, with the walls I built up around me to protect me, unable to communicate with anyone, for there was no one I could trust.

There was no physical enjoyment in our marital relationship either. Our unions gave him pleasure and me children to love, but otherwise it was emotionally and physically painful for me. What has come to light in recent years is the fact I was sexually abused as a small child by my father. It was a question that occasionally haunted me, but I always denied it. Even though I don't have the memories, the evidence is overwhelming and I can't deny it any longer.

Several years ago we moved into a new parish which has Perpetual Adoration. I'm not even sure if I really believed in our Lord's true presence in the Blessed Sacrament at that time, but I signed up for an hour because it just seemed the right thing every Catholic should do. After about six months, I was beginning to think about dropping my hour when I noticed a change. Something was drawing me to the Chapel. For some reason, I began to come early and stay late. Then I signed up for another hour. There was a profound peace there I never experienced before.

Then one evening, as I sat staring at the Monstrance, a great light emanated from it. I was pierced by a Love so intense I remember gasping in pain. During subsequent visits to the

Chapel, this overwhelming Love would continue to consume me. I'd try to meditate but it became a distraction, for the Lord was drawing me into silence. And it was in that silent union with Him that I experienced, for the first time in my life, what Love is, and I couldn't get enough! In this intimate union with Him, He gave me His Heart, and I gave Him mine.

I soon found myself attending daily Mass and daily Adoration, though not understanding what was drawing me there. I began to go to weekly Confession, though I didn't know what to confess. And for the first time in forty years I began to cry... and cry...and cry.

Not having a clue as to what was going on, I sought out a spiritual director. For probably the first year, he did all the talking and I did all the listening. But gradually, for the first time, I began to trust in someone and opened up to him. I've been told that the Holy Spirit has since loosened my tongue.

My husband began to notice my love of the Lord and became extremely possessive and jealous. He began to abuse me—emotionally, physically and sexually. His abuse of me opened up the reality of my abuse as a child. My anger with him exposed the anger deep within toward everyone who had taken advantage of me. Having the lid taken off these festering wounds, the Lord could now work on healing them.

My wounds were deep, and every time I thought I had dealt with my anger, a deeper anger would emerge. I didn't want to face that "dirt" in my "closet" and wanted the door to remain closed; it was ugly and painful. But one night in the chapel I had an image of a jack-in-the-box. The crank would go round and round and up his head would pop, and then I'd stuff him back down again, until he emerged again. I mentioned it to my spiritual director who told me to get my hand off the crank. Without even thinking, I snapped back, "It's not my hand, it's the Lord's." Yes, on this spiritual journey, He is the Great Physician. He wants to uncover all our wounds so He can heal us. St. Teresa says, "He will not give Himself wholly to us until we have given ourselves wholly to Him." We have but to open our hearts and let Him in.

The Lord has brought me on a whirlwind of a journey in just a few short years. The love He has shown me is overwhelming. He's truly been the "Hound of Heaven" and I don't know if I could have escaped Him even if I wanted to. He's brought me through the heights of mystical union and the depths of the Dark Night. He's shared His Sorrowful Heart with me and given me a glimpse of the depths of His Mercy. He's given me an understanding of how scarred we all are, and given me compassion for others in their woundedness.

Through my love for the Lord, and union with Him, He has shown me the spiritual meaning of the marital embrace and the beauty when two give themselves totally to the other. My marriage is on the mend and I pray that it will reach that degree of love and trust.

I'm no longer that rejected, withdrawn, little girl. In the words that my spiritual director drilled into me, "I AM a beloved child of God." He's given new meaning and value to my life for which I am forever grateful.

Thank you, Jesus!

Magdalene

Witness Story on "Disordered Bonds"
Anonymous

It is not clear to me that in every disordered relationship the fault is always on both sides. Perhaps they are typically double-sided, but I am open to one-sided disorders as well. The relationship I am about to describe is the relationship that my wife and I had to my professors in graduate school. It is my opinion that this relationship's disorder was double-sided, although it seems to me the greater responsibility for the disorder was primarily mine, or, I should say, ours. Let me explain.

My wife and I were both twenty-four, just off our honeymoon, when we traveled 1,500 miles for a brand new PhD program. I knew the program was going to be difficult for me because I was going into a new discipline on the doctorate level and I knew that I was both under-prepared and did not have exceptional academic talent. I was going to have to make up for these deficiencies with cold hard work.

What motivated me to turn to this new field was that I heard that this program was taught by serious people who took truth, including religious truth, seriously. I thought these people could be trustworthy while I was "learning the ropes." That first semester I remember reading and re-reading D. von Hildebrand's *What is Philosophy* and coming to the delightful conclusion that philosophy was in no way reducible to mere theories and opinions about it—which interests only philosophical dilettantes—but that people can discover certain truth about important and deep subjects.

Furthermore, my trust in these professors was thoroughly justified. While there were many things that simply "went over my head," the many other things I did receive from them were like gold to me. So I wanted to get through the program, not because I thought I would have any sterling career in philosophy. I was not even confident of even finishing the program, much less of getting a job in philosophy. It is and was incredibly difficult to get an academic position in philosophy. Everyone knew the odds. I stayed in the program because my wife and I knew it was spiritually and academically very good for us to be influenced by these wonderful professors.

The men I studied under were good men, serious Catholics. The integration of their faith with their philosophy was never forced or artificial. It all seemed wondrously of a piece and added to my joy, for after all the truth does not contradict itself.

What a breath of fresh air it was not to have to "check my faith at the door," which is exactly what happened in the psychology graduate program I was in before marriage. The psychology program was for me an academically induced schizophrenia. I was going to daily Mass in the morning and studying secular—if not explicitly atheistic—psychology by the day. Because I myself was trying to become a serious Catholic, I could never make this psychology my own. I was therefore always on the outside looking in. I finally couldn't take it anymore and decided I needed the philosophy instruction for my own mental and spiritual health, even if nothing professional in academic teaching was ever to come of it.

The philosophy program I entered was also different from the psychology program insofar as the philosophy graduate students and professors formed a social and religious community of like-minded people. The relationships between professors and students were much more intimate than practically all other graduate programs. While we were there we considered it a wonderful blessing to be associated with and influenced by these professors.

But as great as this more intimate relation was with these professors, there were inevitably certain drawbacks. The first drawback was that these professors were intellectually brilliant, and one in particular was a philosophical genius. How odd to consider being associated with brilliance and even genius a drawback!

Someone could object in the following way: Think of a world in which you are the morally best and intellectually most gifted person around. Would you want to live in such a world? Of course not. Then how is being associated with brilliance and genius a drawback? It is a drawback insofar as genius is always in your face. For consider, what they grasp simply and immediately you have to struggle to understand or even not understand at all.

Is it worthwhile to humble yourself, to put up with this pain for the sake of their introducing us into a wonderful world of philosophical truth? Oh yes. Does it cease to be painful? Oh no. Someone has said that the only adequate response to a genius is love, because otherwise you would hate him. I can attest to that thought. I even have sympathy for the Pharisees in their relation to Jesus: Putting up with authentic holiness is no easy chore. If you say to me: That's envy! I will completely agree with you, and then tell you that envy makes the world go around. Whole political movements have been formed around envy. It is just beneath the surface with all of us, and it is a movement to health to identify it for the (ugly) little reality it is.

I said at the beginning that our relationship with my professors was disordered on both sides, and so far I have only spoken of my own disorder. Let me mention some mutually influencing disorders. To say that my professors were good, serious men who took the Christian life seriously is not the same as saying they were saints. They were men "on the way," growing up and working out their salvation just like everyone else. And they were young, only a half a dozen years older than my wife and me.

One difficulty I had with one professor in particular was that his sense of humor sometimes "had an edge." It tended towards "chop humor." It is very difficult for someone like me, new to philosophy, insecure, putting this professor on a pedestal and desperately trying to please him, while being on the receiving end of a joke.

Another difficulty was language. My wife and I were exclusively English speakers, while all my professors were either native German speakers or knew the language intimately. Many of the professors and students would go to daily Mass and the time after Mass we would gather and socialize. Invariably during that social time after Mass the switch would be made from English to German, which effectively froze my wife and me out of the discussion. So we would end up standing there in a circle of people feeling utterly stupid and excluded while the others chattered away in German.

We also had religious prayer meetings with our professors in which we would together pray the Divine Office. Unfortunately for us the Divine Office was prayed in Latin, and my wife and I neither knew the Latin nor the Divine Office. We never seemed to figure out where to begin or end, or what we were ever reading. Was this experience good for our humility? Oh yes. Was it painful and humiliating? Oh yes. It is very difficult to be humiliated while at the same time being grateful to them for what they were doing for us.

Naturally, there is no equivalence between the pains and humiliations inflicted upon us with the benefits my professors so generously gave to us. And if we were more mature, the minor disadvantages and problems with my professors could have been minimized. For after all, we could have stuck up for ourselves. We did not have to go to these religious meetings. We did not have to stand there after church and put up with others being, frankly, impolite. We could have simply walked away from the discussion. But we were immature. We were quite capable of being humiliated, but not humble enough to take the jokes in the way they were intended. Our relationship with my professors would have been better and healthier if we were more independent of their approval.

Although my experiences with my professors were very similar to my wife's, in one respect there was the following big difference: I was the graduate student, not her. I was in the favored position. I was the one my professors focused upon and affirmed. I knew they loved me. In contrast, my wife only attended a few of the classes, and never as a formal student. She was mostly out of the mix, either at work or after our children came, staying at home with them. It is only natural that my professors would focus on the student and not the student's wife. After all, my professors, like everyone else, can be drawn in only so many directions. Unfortunately, my wife felt all the humiliations I felt, but without the affirmation I received.

Again, was this philosophy experience worth it? Oh yes. Was it perfect? Well, no. There is no perfection this side of eternity. We simply have to put up with each other.

The events I have so far described took place over twenty-five years ago. I eventually was able to finish graduate school and get a job in philosophy, but we had to move. At first we were upset at leaving the philosophy community that—despite the pain—had been so good to us and for us. We moved to a little Catholic college in the middle of the country where the intellectuals were not orthodox (Catholic) and the orthodox were not particularly intellectual. So we went from a very close-knit religious and intellectual community to practically no community at all. Still, we knew that in God's good time we had to leave.

We had to leave. Oddly enough, for all the goodness of the philosophy community, we left somewhat demoralized; we were perhaps too "under the shadow" of our professors. After we got settled into our new home and in my new career in teaching, I remember remarking jokingly to a fellow teacher how odd it was to be treated with respect by the students. I also remember telling certain students in a class that the "lowest living life form" is certainly a graduate student. Of course such comments were said jokingly and were "over the top." They were, however, exaggerations of how we actually felt.

Perhaps then it is not so surprising that after getting settled in our new situation that upon reflecting on our philosophy graduate program a new experience dawned: anger. Why were we such chumps and groupies? Why didn't we have more self-respect, more emotional distance from the opinions of my professors? Of course we never forgot the tremendous benefits and advantages for us of being exposed to the program and personalities, but that thought only created another difficulty of feeling guilty about being angry towards real benefactors. So despite the loneliness we were grateful for the distance created by the move so as to not have to deal with this complex of emotions.

The time away from the philosophy community was good because it allowed the events of those years to be put in a certain perspective. But while perspective is important, it was alone not enough. For, unfortunately, anger does not have a way of going away. Eventually we had to come not only to understand it, but also to try to forgive them and ourselves for what motivated our anger. Again, forgiving a benefactor is a rather difficult thing to do. It does not come all at once.

There are relationships of love, especially in families, that over the course of a lifetime become so complicated that there seems to be no human way of untying them. Perhaps in principle they could be untied, by exceptional holiness. But in the absence of that all we can do is to beg the dear God to untie them for us. One great sadness of life is the realization that one or another relationship will have to be "fixed" in the next life, insofar as it seems beyond repair in this life. No doubt part of the real joy of heaven is not only seeing God, but also seeing God together with friends and relations where everything is forgiven, fixed and understood.

Another Anonymous Witness

My story involves many traumatic experiences. These have caused me deep anguish, pain and loneliness. I have survived the hurts described here through the gift of courage and through God's providence in giving me a deeply loving wife and children and much success in my work. As well I have experienced many healing graces as a fervent Catholic in prayer and sacramental union and as part of a community that includes committed lay people.

A short account of my early life story will help you understand the context. I was the seventh child in a Catholic family of eight (there were six brothers and two sisters). My parents loved us very much, but they separated when for a time my mother was mentally disturbed. I was then four years old. I saw my parents after that maybe one time in seven years. Psychologists claim that most children sent to foster homes feel rejected, though, of course, I wouldn't have been able to formulate what I felt at such a young age.

Even before the break up of the family, I was very close to Tim, my younger brother. Once when I was four we were left alone. Tim was two years old. I remember taking him by the hand, and crossing the highway to the beauty salon where I believed my mother was. A driver picked us up and took us to the police station. When the police brought us home, I remember everyone laughing and saying we were the youngest outlaws—the police said we were picked up hitchhiking. That little incident bonded me to Tim as did the ultimate challenge to protect him, which came from my older brother the day the social workers came to take us all away to different places.

I can still remember my older brother telling me over and over again, even though I was only four years old, that I should take care of my little brother. I loved him passionately and did everything I could to make him happy. I felt like I had a sacred mission to strengthen and protect my two-year-old brother, and this was a role I took as seriously as life itself. So when we went to the orphanage and ultimately to different foster homes together, you could always find me looking after little Tim. During the fourth grade, I became a member of the safety patrol at school and was recognized as academically gifted.

That year, I became aware that plans were underway for

Timmy's adoption out of this our second foster home. We spent several nights together sleeping and holding on to each other in the same bed, crying and me telling Tim, I would never see him again. Without being able to call it rejection at that time, looking back I see that I was horrified that these foster parents didn't realize that my love for my little brother was much more important than the benefits of having him adopted by another family.

I could not understand why the foster parents thought it was such a good thing that he would have a nice house, a good family, everything he wanted, etc., and I was bad because I was disturbing the transition to this adoption. He was my brother and I loved him, which did not seem to matter. I remember coming home from school one spring afternoon and looking for Tim. I looked everywhere, all over the house and neighborhood, when it hit me that he was gone. That moment numbed me for a very long time; a pain I can still not forget even after all these years.

I guess you might say that my life, already difficult for a boy, became burdened with an existential pain, which I could not shake; he was gone. His death would have been preferable. Death would have seemed more fair and understandable, and final. But I knew he was still alive and I could imagine him in so many ways but could never see him. I was not religious at that time, so I didn't find consolation in prayer.

From that day I stopped producing in school and fell into a life of apathy, the only positive outlet being football and wrestling, which in the long run became very significant for my own growth. I used to love to wrestle because no one could cheat me there. I either won or lost because of my own efforts. No adult, social worker, enemy, or weakling could cheat me of a victory. Although I did not have a father or an older brother to help me— in fact, no one ever came to watch me—I excelled on a team that won the state championship. The discipline I acquired as an athlete I would sorely need as I approached legal maturity.

An interesting twist or irony of life enters here. The third foster home was with a good practicing Catholic Irish family that nurtured me for nine years until I was thirteen. They gave me my love for Notre Dame, where, in spite of all the problems I had in high school I would eventually go to college. All four of their children went to the best prep schools and Catholic schools in Morris County, among the wealthiest counties in the nation. It was the family's desire that their children attend Notre Dame.

I was just a foster child, while the other children went every day to private school, to music lessons, band practice, etc. I stood at the bus stop with my brown lunch bag containing a peanut butter and jelly sandwich, to go to the local public school. I have no memory of help with homework, nor of any parental participation in my athletic events or anything I did. I do remember being physically cared for and having a stable environment during those years for which I am forever grateful. I also remember dropping out after fourth grade, in the sense of becoming apathetic and not doing anything.

Because the foster parents were too strict and I didn't feel loved, I ran away from this family the summer of my freshman year of high school and ended up living with three more families before graduating. I eventually finished 250 out of 252 students in my senior class in spite of sleeping through school, living from prank to prank my senior year, having no goal beyond the immediate, and still suffering deep loss. The day finally came when I turned eighteen and was no longer a ward of the state. That is, the state would no longer provide medical benefits, foster care, food, clothing or anything else. In a word, I was truly all alone. I could be angry and blame everyone or take all my God-given ability and inner pain and turn it toward becoming something good.

It took exactly one crying session in the social worker's office and a moment of realization of the poignancy of the situation for me to wake from my stupor. I cannot say the pain disappeared—in fact, it increased. What I can say is that I began to take care of myself with the deep realization that no one else would, the deep realization that no one else really cared. They wanted to do good and did take care of my needs in a way, but I felt they didn't really know me. I had already acquired the ability to read sincerity of heart and to easily pierce false relationships and human plasticity.

During this time I hung on to the faith in a limited way. I went to Church as a sophomore but not as a junior or senior. The issue at this juncture was if I was going to lay down and die or get up and walk. I decided to walk. Thank God there was a new community college in my neighborhood. I begged to get in, not realizing there was an open door policy. I promised the Dean if accepted I would excel. He helped me get in and I did excel. In three years I graduated with highest honors, a coveted "Scholar Athlete" award, Who's Who, Student Senator, City Intern, etc., a deep yearning to learn more and a burning thirst to go to the University of Notre Dame.

It surely came as a great joy to me and a shock to everyone else when I was accepted at Notre Dame.

With no money, no family, and a rusted 65 Ford Torino, I headed to Notre Dame. In this short piece I can only say that I excelled academically and athletically. But the biggest event was related to the pain I still carried. Yes, I was avoiding it, but it sure came back on cold winter nights when a young man is away from home and reflecting on life. It came back powerfully at a Mexican fiesta in a friend's dormitory room. Deep emotion and tears overcame me that night while telling the others about the loss of my brother Tim so many years ago. The only family member I saw was an older brother who kept in touch and occasionally came to my athletic events. These Notre Dame companions all consoled me. One in particular offered his family's attorney to help find my lost brother. All those friends moved to help in some way.

The following evening, sitting in my dormitory, the phone rang. I thought it was probably my friend calling to discuss the results of his family pow-wow to involve their attorney in seeking my lost brother. I was stunned when the person on the other end asked for me and said, "This is Tim, your brother." He found me because the third family where he was for nine years as a foster child told him where I was.

I met him at his house a mere fifty miles from where I lived in New Jersey. We sat in his room on his bed and hugged each other in tears saying never again would we be parted.

Today Tim is a deacon in the Catholic Church and a Special Agent and Bureau Chief for the FBI. The entire family is reunited. This happened because of studying Jungian therapy in college and having a desire to reconnect with my mother. My father called me because he was in despair. I drove to Miami where they both lived and was able to help him out of that despair. Later on I led the whole family in prayer at my mother's death bed (Tim was not there, but he did come to the funeral), and I am in communion with all my brothers and sisters, some of whom do carry anger and bitterness.

What about anger concerning a traumatic childhood such as mine? Throughout my lifetime, I never was angry with God or my parents. In fact, I revered and honored my parents always, and I deeply loved and honored God, at least as I knew Him. I believe God allowed all this suffering so that I would serve Him in the future, specifically ministering to the lost ones. I am drawn to those on the deep end.

Of course, it is true that one who has suffered a series of setbacks is burdened. This would be true not only because of the pain, but because of other losses suffered, such as perhaps in education not received because of the grieving, or because of lack of funding or support because the family network has been broken, or because of the emotional, social, vocational aptitudes that were not developed as a result of such factors.

People in such a situation are in a seemingly unfair disadvantage and they are mad about this. They might be mad at an abusive parent and this anger spreads because of the failure to develop life skills because of the situation they experience. They might be mad because no one came to their rescue, or ultimately they might be mad at God who permitted such things. When I consider my traumatic childhood, the only anger I think I have concerns people who have tried to understand my pain and have no idea of what they were talking about.

What I am saying is that if we would reexamine each situation, and the reasons for the situation, we should be able to identify the proper emotion, which should be elicited. Anger is an emotion, which is justified as a result of a conscious wrong purposefully done to hurt someone. If a father abuses a child because he gets a kick out of it or abandons a family because he finds another situation more attractive, I suppose anger is an appropriate response, and in fact, a response that need not ever go away because the situation deserves anger—it is the appropriate response. But if that anger generalizes to others it can be inappropriate.

In most cases, though, I think the reason for a general angry stance toward others throughout life comes from an over emphasis on the self, that is a solipsistic self-love mixed with a pride of life, which makes debilitating circumstances result in anger because one is at a loss vis a vis others who have not suffered such a loss. It is as if the setbacks of life are one's excuse for not achieving his/her potential.

Irene

I asked this woman, single, around forty years of age, to write an account of rejection and how God has helped her in it. So far, she hasn't written a formal piece but I would like to quote some ramblings about it she sent me. The writer is a woman who experienced psychological rejection from both parents in a severe manner leading to anorexia in her teens and bulimia later on. She has been through many kinds of psychotherapy.

Rejection. This is a theme that came up over and over

again. I've promised to write about it. I've some thoughts on it, but every time I think about writing, it seems that more surfaces.

I realize that rejection, like loneliness, is a universal human experience—all of us have been met with rejection at some point, but some of us have a deeper share in it. But I think it is more than a feeling— it is often a real experience, something we suffer that stirs up a little brew of emotions, which, left untended, can become a rather pussy sort of wound. It is at the root, for so many including me, of self-pity, resentment, bitterness, shame, fear and the inability to trust, feelings of inferiority or unworthiness.

In psychology one often hears it referred to as a "feeling." In this, psychology falls very short: it might be a cause of skewed thinking or painful emotions, but it is fundamentally a wound of the heart. Healing the wound of rejection begins on the level of the heart, the core of our being and more primary than our rationality.

Perhaps Conrad Baars was thinking of rejection too when he wrote about the lack of affirmation. Certainly, his understanding of affirmation, of being received unconditionally (or affirmed, as he says), simply for who you are, is closely related. To the extent that we are affirmed, or know ourselves consciously and subconsciously, to be rooted in love, we are less prone to becoming wounded by the experience of rejection.

But for me, rejection, deep rejection, goes back to such an early age—before I can remember really. I think the best way to describe the experience is in the etymology of the word itself: to be thrown back onto oneself.

It was not something I blame anyone for: all of us bear wounds from childhood. And, it was never a comfort to me that Christ too felt this way—that he too experienced rejection and bore those wounds himself. It takes, I think, a kind of experiencing—or reexperiencing rejection—in and through Christ and allowing first the anger, then the fear, shame and even guilt underneath the anger to be exposed. Only then can I realize that Christ did in fact experience real rejection—and to such an infinitely greater extent because his love is infinite.

Christ did really suffer most deeply from rejection, since he is love itself. He reached out to us to make it graspable, to make plain to us the lengths and depths of his love and to give us what our own hearts were longing for.

Not only do we reject, but the wounds to his own heart were so much more piercing because his heart was so much more tender. So, I think that to be rejected means that the love my heart naturally tends toward in reaching out to others, both to give and, in giving, to receive, is not for me. Instead, there is nothing but bitter isolation. In the end, I am not a gift; I am nothing at all. There is no hope for meaning. I am nothing.

To be a gift I must first be received, be welcomed as such. But if I am not received, my gift—the gift of myself—is worthless. Love (the gift of self) or the kind of reciprocal love that we are made for, is a relationship. Rejection in the deepest sense is a refusal of all of this. This is why the rejection of Christ cannot be underestimated.

We are made through him out of sheer gratuitous love. He delights in the existence of each one. The image of being thrown back on myself, touches, for me, on one of the deepest existential fears I have had—a fear of annihilation, which is worse than death. (In death, there is still some hope—ps 139—Whither can I go from your spirit, or whither shall I flee from thy presence? If I ascend to the heaven, thou art there! If I make my bed in Sheol, thou art there!)

But the fear of annihilation is the fear that the love that holds me in existence will be withdrawn and then I will cease to be. Obviously there are degrees of rejection, and I don't think anyone is ever immune to the experience. But the antidote is knowing oneself as irrevocably rooted in God's love, and even more, knowing beyond the hint of any doubt that God, by his very nature, cannot ever withdraw his love.

So even in the "little" rejections, the ones we experience when we are shut out of the company of friends or family in some way, is an opportunity to be as children of God and run to him with the fear, the hurt. This doesn't make it easy. Worse yet, and I think, among the worst, is a rejection by someone to whom you unconditionally give yourself—usually a lover or spouse.

But I think this can be the case with close friends too. And this can come in many forms. Sometimes it is the realization that you have been used, and your generosity of heart exploited. Sometimes it is a perceived rejection. Sometimes rejection comes when you have "thrown your pearls to the dogs" and on and on. And always, with rejection, there is grief, the loss of something you think is essential to your very self. And again, and through the love of God we can come to know and experience ourselves as having no lack or need, but only opportunities for His love to create and recreate and be made manifest through us. But these are my ramblings on rejection.

www.ingramcontent.com/pod-product-compliance
Lightning Source LLC
Chambersburg PA
CBHW031849090426
42741CB00005B/422